Early Keyboard Instruments

Early Keyboard Instruments covers a wide range of performance issues
on keyboard instruments relevant to music from the seventeenth to the
nineteenth century. It includes descriptions of the harpsichords,
clavichords, pianos and other stringed keyboard instruments used by
performers of the period as well as aspects of technique such as
harpsichord registration, piano pedalling and keyboard fingering. Aspects
of the notation of keyboard music are discussed, as are matters such as
articulation, embellishment, tempo flexibility and rubato. A substantial
chapter is devoted to case studies, illustrating how the aspects of
performance discussed in the rest of the book are worked out in practice,
whether playing on period instruments or on the modern piano. A select
bibliography and extensive endnotes enable the reader to take all of the
issues further.

DAVID ROWLAND is Senior Lecturer in Music at the Open University
and Director of Music at Christ's College, Cambridge. He has made
frequent broadcasts and recordings as an organist, harpsichordist and
fortepianist and is author of *A History of Pianoforte Pedalling* (1993) and
editor of *The Cambridge Companion to the Piano* (1998).

Cambridge Handbooks to the Historical Performance of Music

GENERAL EDITORS: Colin Lawson and Robin Stowell

During the last three decades historical performance has become part of mainstream musical life. However, there is as yet no one source from which performers and students can find an overview of the significant issues or glean practical information pertinent to a particular instrument. This series of handbooks guides the modern performer towards the investigation and interpretation of evidence found both in early performance treatises and in the mainstream repertory. Books on individual instruments contain chapters on historical background, equipment, technique and musical style and are illustrated by case studies of significant works in the repertoire. An introductory book provides a more general survey of issues common to all areas of historical performance and will also inform a wide range of students and music lovers.

Published titles

COLIN LAWSON AND ROBIN STOWELL *The Historical Performance of Music: An Introduction*

COLIN LAWSON *The Early Clarinet: A Practical Guide*

JOHN HUMPHRIES *The Early Horn: A Practical Guide*

DAVID ROWLAND *Early Keyboard Instruments: A Practical Guide*

ROBIN STOWELL *The Early Violin and Viola: A Practical Guide*

Forthcoming

RACHEL BROWN *The Early Flute: A Practical Guide*

Early Keyboard Instruments
A Practical Guide

David Rowland

CAMBRIDGE
UNIVERSITY PRESS

PUBLISHED BY THE PRESS SYNDICATE OF THE UNIVERSITY OF CAMBRIDGE
The Pitt Building, Trumpington Street, Cambridge, United Kingdom

CAMBRIDGE UNIVERSITY PRESS
The Edinburgh Building, Cambridge CB2 2RU, UK
40 West 20th Street, New York NY 10011-4211, USA
10 Stamford Road, Oakleigh, VIC 3166, Australia
Ruiz de Alarcón 13, 28014 Madrid, Spain
Dock House, The Waterfront, Cape Town 8001, South Africa

http://www.cambridge.org

First published 2001

Printed in the United Kingdom at the University Press, Cambridge

Typeface Adobe Minion 10.25/14 pt.   *System* QuarkXPress™   [SE]

A catalogue record for this book is available from the British Library

Library of Congress Cataloguing in Publication data

Rowland, David, Dr.
Early keyboard instruments: a practical guide / David Rowland.
    p.   cm. – (Cambridge handbooks to the historical performance of music)
Includes bibliographical references and indexes.
ISBN 0 521 64366 X (hardback) – ISBN 0 521 64385 6 (paperback)
1. Keyboard instruments.   2. Keyboard instrument music – History and
criticism.   3. Performance practice (Music)   I. Title.   II. Series.
ML549.R69   2001
786′.19 – dc21   00-062179

ISBN 0 521 64366 X hardback
ISBN 0 521 64385 6 paperback

Contents

vii

Preface

As the title of the volume suggests, this is an introduction to playing historical keyboard instruments rather than a comprehensive survey of the subject.
Aspects of all of the topics covered here have been treated in greater detail
elsewhere and it is part of the purpose of the volume to direct readers
towards the specialist literature by means of the endnotes and Select
Bibliography. In particular, a number of issues that are only touched upon
here (such as double dotting, *inégales*, etc.) are explored in Colin Lawson
and Robin Stowell's *The historical performance of music: an introduction*
(Cambridge University Press, 1999), the introductory volume to this series.

The historical scope of this study reflects that of the series to which it
belongs. The reader will therefore find a range of topics relevant to the performance of music from the seventeenth to the nineteenth century. The
study is restricted to performance practices relating to stringed keyboard
instruments. This is not because the techniques of early organ playing are
fundamentally different from those of stringed keyboard instruments –
most early keyboard players included the organ in the range of instruments
upon which they performed. However, organ performance does raise a
number of issues that are irrelevant to other keyboard instruments, issues
not just to do with the instrument itself, but also relating to the context in
which the instrument was used. A line had to be drawn somewhere, and in
such a condensed study it seemed sensible to leave out any specific mention
of the organ altogether.

In the preparation of this volume I have received help from a number of
people. I would particularly like to thank Penny Souster, of Cambridge
University Press, for her help, patience and advice through the process.
Special thanks are also due to Colin Lawson and Robin Stowell, general
editors of the series, for their advice in the early stages, and for their comments on drafts of the volume. A number of others have read parts of the
volume at various stages of its preparation – Donald Burrows, Richard

Maunder and Christopher Stembridge – and I am grateful to them for their help. I have also had many interesting and informative conversations with instrument makers, restorers and tuners, especially Alan Gotto, David Hunt and Andrew Wooderson. Blaise Compton deserves thanks for his assistance in the preparation of the musical examples. Finally, I would like to record my appreciation of the patient role played by my wife, Ruth, and daughters Kate, Hannah and Eleanor throughout the venture.

Abbreviations and pitch nomenclature

EKJ *Early Keyboard Journal*
EM *Early Music*
GSJ *Galpin Society Journal*
ML *Music & Letters*
MQ *Musical Quarterly*
MT *Musical Times*
PPR *Performance Practice Review*
PRMA *Proceedings of the Royal Musical Association*

Pitches are referred to as follows:

The standard abbreviation has been adopted for short octaves:
C/E means that the pitch C sounds on the key that usually plays
E at the bottom of the keyboard.

1 Stylistic awareness and keyboard music

It is a common assumption among musicians that certain performing styles are appropriate to particular parts of the repertory, or to the music of individual composers. It would be difficult to imagine, for example, a Baroque dance movement or a Mozart sonata being played by any modern performer in the same manner as a Liszt fantasia: there appears to be a consensus that the degree of dynamic variation, rhythmic flexibility and so on should vary according to the style of the music being played. This is true of those who use modern instruments as well as those who play on originals, or copies of historic instruments. But how and when did this stylistic awareness develop?

It was in the eighteenth century that 'old' music – the music of previous generations – came to be performed regularly in a variety of contexts. Performance of 'old' music went hand in hand with its publication and with the writing of some of the earliest histories of music. Exactly how and where this happened is described in Lawson and Stowell's book, and elsewhere.[1] Inevitably, as 'old' music was played, questions were raised about its performance.

Louis Adam was among the first writers on the performance of keyboard music to comment on historical styles in his *Méthode de piano du conservatoire* (Paris, 1804). The final chapter of Adam's *Méthode* is devoted to a discussion of the subject. His argument is not developed at length, but he nevertheless points out that Bach and Handel each had a unique style of performance, and that any pianist who plays the music of Clementi, Mozart, Dussek and Haydn in the same way will destroy the music's effect.[2] A similar, but more detailed argument is made in Czerny's keyboard tutor, Op. 500 (1839), in a chapter headed 'on the peculiar style of execution most suitable to different composers and their works'. Among Czerny's conclusions were the observation that 'in the commencement of the eighteenth century, the legato style of playing . . . had already been carried to a high degree of perfection by *Seb. Bach*, Domenico Scarlatti, and others'. He divided pianists of the eighteenth and early nineteenth centuries into 'principal schools', each defined by its own characteristic performance style. 'Mozart's school' was characterised by 'a distinct and considerably brilliant manner of playing, calculated rather on the Staccato than on the Legato touch; an intelligent and animated execution, The Pedal seldom used, and never obligato'. 'Beethoven's style' was different: 'characteristic and impassioned energy, alternating with all the charms of smooth and connected cantabile, is in its place here. The means of Expression is often carried to excess, particularly in regard to humourous and fanciful levity.' Other 'schools' identified by Czerny were 'Clementi's style', 'Cramer and Dussek's style', 'the modern brilliant school' of 'Hummel, Kalkbrenner and Moscheles' and the 'new style' of 'Thalberg, Chopin, Liszt and other young artists'.[3]

Czerny's research into early performance history can hardly be described as rigorous, but his reading of the sources available to him was sufficient to give him a general understanding of stylistic matters, sufficient to persuade him that early keyboard music needed its own performance style. However, like other musicians of the period (and like many pianists today), his concern for stylistic appropriateness was tempered by an urge to up-date earlier music.

Virtually all of the authors who wrote on the history of instruments and their performance in the nineteenth century did so from a perspective of a firm belief in the notion of progress. The piano was seen as an 'advance' on the harpsichord and the changes in the piano's action that took place in the period were described as 'improvements'. It would have been illogical for musicians who thought in this way to do anything other than up-date earlier music. The approach can be seen even in Czerny's detailed observations on the way in which the music of his revered master, Beethoven, was to be played. In places, Czerny advocated changes in the composer's performing directions in order to accommodate the qualities of more modern pianos. Of a passage from the slow movement of Beethoven's Third Piano Concerto, for example, he wrote:

> Beethoven (who publicly played this Concerto in 1803) continued the pedal during the entire theme, which on the weak-sounding pianofortes of that day, did very well, especially when the shifting

pedal [una corda] was also employed. But now, as the instruments
have acquired a much greater body of tone, we should advise the
damper pedal to be employed anew, at each important change of
harmony.[4]

The urge to up-date and a sense that earlier music should be played in a way
that exhibited some sense of stylistic awareness are both features of music
editions from the end of the eighteenth and the first half of the nineteenth
centuries. Clementi's edition of some of Scarlatti's sonatas as *Scarlatti's chef-
d'œuvre* in 1791, for example, included the addition of many dynamic markings (*p*, *f*, *fz*, *cresc.*, *dim.*, etc.) as well as terms such as 'dolce' and a few
articulation markings. Nevertheless, Clementi's overall approach as an
editor was one of restraint, compared with the level of dynamic and articulation markings found in his own works of the same period. For his own
piano tutor, the *Introduction* of 1801, Clementi adopted an even less inter-
ventionist editorial stance. Works by Corelli, Handel, Rameau, Couperin
and Scarlatti appear with few, if any, dynamic or other markings – a trend
followed in numerous other piano tutors of the early nineteenth century.

Czerny's editions of Bach's music are full of dynamic, accent, articulation
and phrase markings, with occasional additional notes to fill out the texture,
such as the added bass octaves in the closing few bars of the C minor fugue
from Book 1 of the '48'. However, such markings should not necessarily be
seen to be at variance with his comments on performance style in his tutor:
Czerny was more restrained than many of his contemporaries, who showed
a marked disregard for notions of stylistic awareness. The trend reached a
peak towards the end of the nineteenth century and in the first decades of
the twentieth, a period in which some remarkable 'editions' of early keyboard works were published. These 'editions' are in reality adaptations or
arrangements. The music is sometimes transposed into a new key, passages
are re-written and numerous performance directions are added. Among the
more extreme examples are Tausig's and von Bülow's editions of Scarlatti
and Busoni's editions of Bach. Example 1.2 is Busoni's reworking of the final
statement of the theme from Bach's 'Goldberg Variations' (Ex. 1.1).

While most pianists were either performing with some degree of stylistic
awareness, or showing no regard at all for historical performance issues, a
few musicians were beginning to investigate early keyboard practices more

Ex. 1.1 J. S. Bach, 'Goldberg Variations', Aria, bars 1–4

Ex. 1.2 Busoni's arrangement of Ex. 1.1

carefully and it is in the work of these individuals that the origins of the modern 'historical performance movement' lie.

The 1830s saw the beginning of a long line of 'historical performances'. Fétis organised what were probably the first concerts of their kind in Paris during the autumn and winter of 1832–3.[5] The programmes comprised music of many kinds – opera, vocal and instrumental – and early instruments were used, including the harpsichord. In the years 1837–8 Moscheles organised a series of concerts which were specifically designed to demonstrate the wealth of keyboard styles of the past and present. The reviewer of the first concert observed that

> one circumstance at the conclusion of the entertainment particularly struck us, and that was, the manner in which Mr. Moscheles threw himself into the various character of the music he was playing. The style in which he executed a fugue of Bach, and a florid finale of Weber or Beethoven, was so perfectly according with the genius, and we should suppose the intention of each composer, as if he had studied in this school alone.[6]

Moscheles' concern for stylistic propriety extended to the use of a harpsichord (a 1771 5½-octave instrument by Shudi[7]) in several of his concerts.

He apparently thought that Scarlatti's music was particularly idiomatic to the harpsichord, since his programmes frequently featured the composer's sonatas played on the instrument. He played Bach's preludes and fugues on the piano, however, perhaps because by that time Bach was known to have given his approval to some of Silbermann's early pianos (see Chapter 3), or perhaps simply because the preludes and fugues had been appropriated by so many pianists that they were regarded as piano music.

Fétis' and Moscheles' interest in historical performance styles is evident in their jointly authored *Méthode des Méthodes de Piano* (Paris, 1840). The text of the *Méthode* makes it clear that the performance of keyboard repertory requires a variety of approaches, depending on the composer of any particular work, and the tutor is liberally footnoted with references to keyboard treatises from C. P. E. Bach onwards. Illustrative of the extent of the authors' concern for stylistic propriety are their views on ornamentation: readers are told that modern ornaments are not necessarily appropriate to earlier music, and they are advised to familiarise themselves with the contemporary meanings of ornament signs in the music of Couperin, Bach, Handel, Clementi, Mozart and others.[8] Here we see the beginnings of the study of performance practice based on keyboard treatises of the past, and it was not long before some attention was given to the re-publication of some of the major tutors. The first appears to have been a heavily edited version (by Gustav Schilling) of C. P. E. Bach's *Versuch*, in the 1850s. Others followed only gradually: Couperin's important *L'Art de toucher le clavecin*, for example, was not published until 1933.

The concern to understand the notation and performance conventions of early keyboard music went hand in hand with the systematic publication, from the second half of the nineteenth century, of a great deal of early keyboard music. Some of this repertory, such as Bach's '48' and selections of Scarlatti's sonatas, had been available in print from around the turn of the century. Much more of it became known through the publication of composers' complete works, beginning in Germany with Breitkopf & Härtel's edition of Bach's music, published from 1851, and followed by the complete works of Handel (from 1858), Mozart (from 1877) and others. The trend was followed elsewhere: at the end of the century, for example, the works of Rameau were published in France. Anthologies were also an important means of making early keyboard music known. One of the most significant was Farrenc's *Le trésor des pianistes*, published in Paris in the years 1861–72, which included works by composers such as Byrd, Bull, Gibbons, Merulo, Frescobaldi and many later composers.[9]

As a greater amount of early keyboard music circulated among performers, so an interest in hearing the music performed on early instruments grew. More historical recitals were given in the middle of the century, including those organised in London by Salaman (from 1855) and Pauer (from 1861 – using the same harpsichord as Moscheles)[10] – and in Paris by Diémer (from the mid 1860s).[11] At around the same time, the foundations for some of the most important collections of historic keyboard instruments were laid. Several individuals built private collections which were later given to, or purchased by, institutions and some institutions themselves began to collect. Around the middle of the nineteenth century, collections such as those now in the Victoria and Albert Museum, the Royal College of Music, the Brussels and Paris Conservatoires, the Berlin Musikinstrumenten-Museum, the Leipzig University Musikinstrumenten-Sammlung, the New York Metropolitan Museum of Art and the Washington Smithsonian Institution were formed.[12]

By the 1880s interest in early keyboard instruments had become widespread. In 1885, Alfred Hipkins organised an exhibition of about a hundred historic keyboard instruments with the assistance of William Dale.[13] This was followed four years later by one of the most important events in the history of the harpsichord revival – the Paris Exposition – which marked the beginnings of modern harpsichord making. Tomasini, Erard and Pleyel all exhibited new harpsichords at the 1889 Paris Exposition. These instruments were in part the fruits of restoration work previously carried out in Paris. Charles Fleury had been restoring harpsichords as early as the 1850s,[14] but more important in the harpsichord revival than Fleury was Louis Tomasini, who in 1882 restored the 1769 Taskin harpsichord used by Diémer for his historical recitals (the instrument is now in the Russell Collection, Edinburgh).[15] Following the instrument's restoration, Erard and Pleyel borrowed it for study prior to making their own. However, neither maker produced exact copies and Tomasini himself chose to base his new instrument on an eighteenth-century Parisian harpsichord by Hemsch.[16]

The three 1889 Exposition harpsichords are now in the Berlin Staatliches Institut für Musikforschung.[17] All of the instruments are highly decorated and some features, such as the black natural and white sharp keys of the Tomasini and Erard harpsichords, suggest that these instruments resemble the eighteenth-century models used for study by their makers. However, only Tomasini's instrument is constructed on anything like eighteenth-century principles. Erard's and Pleyel's instruments have a much heavier internal structure than their 'models' and the adoption of registration pedals by Pleyel is another thoroughly modern feature.

The modernisation of harpsichord design was the predominant feature of harpsichord making between 1890 and the end of the Second World War.[18] An impressive collection of examples by French and German makers can be seen in the Berlin Staatliches Institut collection. The overriding concerns of makers in this period were the production of sufficient volume for the modern concert platform and the provision of more colouristic possibilities than were customary on earlier instruments. Hence, the construction of harpsichords was heavy, sometimes involving metal frame members, and the choice of registers was plentiful, with pedals for changing registration quickly. These were the harpsichords played by the early modern exponents of the instrument, among them Wanda Landowska, Violet Gordon Woodhouse and others.

After the Second World War a few makers began to construct harpsichords according to historical principles. Among the most important of these individuals were Hugh Gough, Frank Hubbard and William Dowd. Most makers now follow this approach.

Much of the nineteenth- and early twentieth-century revival of interest in early keyboards, their technique and their repertory centred on the harpsichord. It is only more recently that widespread interest in the clavichord and early piano has become established, although there are several instances of performances on both types of instrument at surprisingly early dates. In fact, it can be argued that there was an unbroken tradition of clavichord playing in the nineteenth century.[19] However, fresh impetus was gained in c. 1857 when Hoffmann of Stuttgart made a clavichord for an English amateur, Joseph Street, and a number of individuals including Hipkins and Engel showed considerable interest in the instrument.[20]

The early piano initially fared no better than the clavichord.[21] A few early performances took place, such as those presented by the fortepiano society formed around 1906 in Munich. These ventures generated little general enthusiasm, however, and performances on early pianos generally suffered from the poor state of preservation of old instruments and invidious comparison with modern piano playing. In the second half of the twentieth century this situation changed very markedly. Owing to the performances of individuals such as Paul Badura-Skoda, Malcolm Bilson and more recently Melvyn Tan, as well as the efforts of restorers and makers of reproduction instruments such as Derek Adlam and Philip Belt, audiences are now much more appreciative of the qualities of early pianos.

2   Repertory, performance and notation

Choice and sources of repertory

A particular problem associated with the choice of keyboard repertory is the sheer quantity of music available. In each century of keyboard music history there have been several major keyboard composers, as well as dozens of minor figures who wrote works that are worthy of modern performance. More and more of this repertory is becoming available in editions and in facsimile.

It is possible to select repertory in at least two fundamentally different ways. Many of the best-known performers have made their names by specialising in the music of a composer, or period, because they have had a particular empathy with certain works, because they have had access to instruments that are suited to part of the repertory, or for some other reason. A second and much more usual approach is to choose a representative sample of music by several composers from a variety of periods. Performers who adopt this approach inevitably draw on works from the mainstream repertory – music that is most frequently recorded and heard in concerts.[1]

A choice of works from the mainstream repertory is unlikely to raise eyebrows. Realistically, most performers will have to play this repertory in order to secure some credibility. However, 'mainstream repertory' is not necessarily the same as 'the best repertory'. There are several reasons why some works, and not others, have come to the fore, and these reasons have as much to do with the historical availability of music as with its enduring quality, as the following paragraphs briefly show.

The music that was available to keyboard players before the eighteenth century included their own compositions as well as whatever repertory they could accumulate in manuscript, or purchase from the relatively small number of publications that were accessible. During the eighteenth century, especially towards its close, the music publishing industry expanded very rapidly. Not only did contemporary works appear in print, but a few selected works by earlier composers began to be published. For example, by the end of the eighteenth century Bach's '48', some of Scarlatti's sonatas and certain of Handel's 'lessons' were readily available. However, other works such as Bach's 'French' or 'English' suites and much of Handel's and Scarlatti's music remained in manuscript and was seldom performed. Perhaps even more significantly, only a tiny proportion of keyboard music by any earlier composers was available.

By the second half of the nineteenth century keyboard players had access to a much greater body of keyboard music. The complete works of a number of composers were published along with some substantial anthologies. Despite the volume of publication, however, the process inevitably remained selective and some significant parts of the repertory were under-represented – such as the earlier keyboard music of France, Italy, Austria and some other parts of continental Europe. Meanwhile, judgements were formed on the relative significance of works and composers. These judgements were expressed in a variety of ways; by the inclusion of works in keyboard tutors, anthologies, in historical recitals, and in the syllabuses of conservatories and other institutions. Histories of the piano and its music were also influential in shaping opinions about repertory. Early influential histories of repertory were those by Prosniz, Bie and Seiffert, all written at the end of the nineteenth century.[2]

In the twentieth century the notion of what constituted the mainstream repertory was reinforced by the recording industry. During the early decades of the century many 'core' works were recorded, such as the complete cycle of Beethoven's sonatas, but it was not until very much later that something of the real breadth of the keyboard repertory was represented in the recording catalogues.[3]

To a large extent the nineteenth- and early twentieth-century judgements about what constituted 'mainstream repertory' continue to inform the repertory choices of modern keyboard players. However, with the increasing availability of editions and recordings of hitherto little-known music it is evident that there are parts of the repertory that are unjustifiably under-represented in modern performances. There is plenty of good keyboard music to explore outside of the confines of the 'mainstream repertory' and information about this extended repertory will be found in two main types of source.

The first main source of information about repertory includes catalogues and general surveys, of which there are several. Some of the most useful and accessible that are available in the English language are listed in the Select Bibliography at the end of this volume, including those by Apel, Caldwell, Gustafson (and Fuller), Harley, Marshall, Newman, Silbiger and Todd.

The second type of source is the music itself, particularly the multi-volume collections of keyboard music that are available. Most of the works of major composers can be found in complete editions of their music, although many of these editions are as yet unfinished. In addition, the music of lesser-known figures is found in a number of multi-volume collections.[4] A number of smaller anthologies also exist and are mentioned in the bibliographies of some of the repertory surveys listed in the Select Bibliography and at the end of *The New Grove* article 'Keyboard music'.[5]

Repertories, performance traditions and keyboard tutors

The keyboard repertory is divided into a number of different 'schools' according to period and geographical region. These 'schools' were often associated with a distinctive style of performance. An appreciation of some of the general issues associated with the performance styles of these different 'schools' is essential for modern performers.

Before the middle of the nineteenth century instrument design varied from country to country, and sometimes within national boundaries: a description of the major differences will be found in the next chapter. Composers were often acutely aware of a particular keyboard instrument's character and qualities and wrote accordingly. It is important for modern performers to take these factors into consideration when preparing stylish performances.

It is possible, however, to be overly concerned with having the 'right' instrument. Attempts to identify a single instrument, or type of instrument, with any work or repertory can ignore the fact that the composers, who usually performed the music themselves, did not necessarily play the same type of instrument all of the time. Musicians often travelled – Froberger, for example, spent time in Austria, Italy and France, Handel worked in Germany, Italy and England, Mozart travelled widely throughout Europe, and so on. But musicians did not necessarily have to travel abroad to play foreign instruments. From early on in the development of keyboard instruments, makers sent examples of their workmanship abroad, despite the obvious problems of transporting such bulky items. Italian instruments are generally thought to have been well-known in many parts of Europe from the sixteenth to the eighteenth centuries, for example,[6] and Ruckers harpsichords and spinets were widely used outside of the Netherlands in the seventeenth and eighteenth centuries.[7] Some of the earliest Italian pianos were found as far afield as England, and later eighteenth- and early-nineteenth-century English pianos were known all over Europe, in the United States and elsewhere around the world.[8]

Just as instrument design varied from country to country, so did other aspects of performance. Different styles of ornamentation and embellishment were practised in France, Italy and elsewhere. Rhythmic conventions such as over-dotting and *notes inégales* were peculiar to certain regions in certain periods.[9] But to what extent were these practices confined to the geographical areas in which they originated?

Since musicians travelled throughout the period under investigation here, it is reasonable to conjecture that their performance styles travelled with them, and that they adopted certain of the styles that they found in foreign countries. Italy is particularly important in this regard, since for several centuries Italian musicians travelled and worked widely in Europe. Italy was also a destination for many musicians (including figures such as Handel and Mozart) who often went there with a view to broadening their musical education. It is no wonder, therefore, that the Italian style proved to be so important, especially in the seventeenth and eighteenth centuries. To a lesser extent, France was also influential. In an attempt to mimic the splendour of the French court, several European rulers created musical establishments resembling the '24 violons du Roi' of Louis XIV. Charles II attempted to do just this on his return to London in the 1660s and Bach's familiarity with the French-style court of Celle in North Germany is well known.

Despite the cultural interaction that must have taken place, however, we cannot assume that the majority of musicians from the seventeenth to the early nineteenth century would have been entirely familiar with a wide variety of performance traditions. If this had been the case, it would be difficult to account for publications such as Muffat's *Florilegium secundum*,[10] which attempted to describe the major characteristics of French and

Italian performance traditions, presumably for musicians who had no direct experience of them.

Temporal and regional differences in performance styles are reflected in the hundreds of performance tutors that were written, some of them specific to the keyboard and others of more general interest. Although the tutors are numerous, they are not of equal use: many are brief and of a very elementary nature. This is particularly true of nineteenth-century keyboard tutors, of which over 200 were published in the first half of the century alone. Nevertheless, the more substantial tutors are a vital source for our knowledge of earlier performance practices and historians of the subject have relied heavily on them. A list of some of the most informative and influential keyboard tutors of the seventeenth, eighteenth and nineteenth centuries appears in the Select Bibliography. The list also includes a few important tutors for other instruments that contain important information of a general nature. Other tutors are listed by Jackson, and Vinquist and Zaslaw.[11]

Like all sources, performance manuals need to be treated with care. Some important questions need to be asked of them: Why did the author write the work? For whom was it written? To what period does it refer? How far does it represent widespread practices, or does it reflect only local trends? Only by asking questions such as these can the reader avoid some serious pitfalls.[12] The way in which C. P. E. Bach's *Versuch*[13] has been used in the past illustrates some of the problems. Because Bach's tutor was the first keyboard manual to be re-published and translated in modern times (see Chapter 1), and because it contains so much detailed information, it became enormously influential in twentieth-century discussions of performance practice. However, some writers appealed to it for evidence of performance practices with which Bach cannot possibly have been familiar. Bach's comments on overdotting, for example, have been used as evidence for earlier French Baroque practices[14] and his remarks about continuo practice have been taken as normative for the late seventeenth and early eighteenth centuries (see Chapter 7). Yet Bach's tutor was published after 1750 and it was written by a musician who can only have had limited experience of non-German practices. Valuable though it is in many ways, Bach's tutor must be read as a document that reflects first and foremost performance practices in Berlin in the middle of the eighteenth century.

Fig. 2.1 Charles Hallé's edition (*c.* 1866) of the B♭ minor fugue from Book I of J. S. Bach's 48 Preludes and Fugues

Although primary sources such as tutors have enormous value for performers, it is important that the information contained in them is balanced against a much wider range of evidence. There is a growing literature on the subject, some of it relating to general performance issues and some of it relating specifically to the keyboard. The general literature is discussed at some length in the introductory volume to this series by Lawson and Stowell.[15] Important studies of keyboard-related issues may be found in the literature listed in the Select Bibliography at the end of this volume.

Editions and facsimiles

Of the enormous range of editions that is available to keyboard players, some convey the composers' intentions faithfully while others overlay the original musical text with suggestions for performance, or even make changes to the notes themselves. As Chapter 1 pointed out, the period that saw the most extreme variation in approaches to editing was the late nineteenth and early twentieth centuries. Most editions at that time updated the music to a greater or lesser degree: the most extreme examples amount to virtual re-composition of works (see Exx. 1.1, 1.2) while others are characterised by a profusion of performance directions – Figure 2.1 is a heavily-edited version of Bach's 'clean' text (Ex. 2.1). However, at the same

Ex. 2.1 J. S. Bach, Fugue in B♭ minor from Book I of the 48 Preludes and Fugues, bars 1–6

time a more scholarly approach was being developed which is particularly evident in the series of collected editions that began with the publication of Bach's works by the Bach-Gesellschaft in the 1850s. Many of these collected editions are now available in inexpensive photo-reproductions published by firms such as Kalmus and Dover. They remain a very useful resource.

An important characteristic of the Bach edition, which was taken up by subsequent editors of collected editions, was its critical approach to sources. Each of the volumes of music in the series was accompanied by a *kritischer Bericht* (critical commentary) which discusses in greater or lesser detail the sources available to the editor (typically including the composer's autograph, early manuscript copies and any relevant first edition) and their variant readings. Another characteristic of these early collected editions is their relatively 'clean' appearance – editorial interventions are usually kept to a minimum and, consequently, suggestions for modern performance are few. However, the extent to which these principles were adhered to was not uniform: some editors grasped the new scholarly approach better than others. Whereas, for example, the music of Bach and Handel was usually edited to the highest standards of the day in the volumes of the old Breitkopf & Härtel complete editions, that of Mozart was often given additional phrasing and other performance directions.

The study of early sources expanded greatly in the twentieth century, leading to a second wave of complete editions from the middle of the century, including the *Neue Bach-Ausgabe, Neue Mozart-Ausgabe* (both published by Bärenreiter) and others. These editions, and those that have been completed to a similar editorial standard, usually offer modern performers the best available performing text. In order to make full use of these modern scholarly editions it is necessary to understand something of the role of the editor. The issues are discussed at greater length by Lawson and Stowell, Caldwell, Grier and others:[16] only a brief summary is given here.

Editors first have to decide which source to choose as the basis for an edition. This may be difficult, since it is not unusual for sources to exist of a

Ex. 2.2 W.A. Mozart, Sonata, K.332, slow movement, bars 23–4 (the composer's autograph)

Ex. 2.3 W.A. Mozart, Sonata, K.332, slow movement, bars 23–4 (first edition)

work at various stages of its genesis. The establishment of a preferred text may be problematic, since it is not always obvious which source represents the most definitive thoughts of the composer. Indeed, the composer may not have had any 'definitive thoughts' about a piece – a particular problem with Chopin, for example, who frequently revised his works (see Chapter 6). Decisions about sources are explained in the critical commentaries of scholarly editions, which often illuminate the way in which a composer thought about a work.

There are cases where two or more performable versions of a work cannot be reconciled. Bach's *French Overture*, for which two versions exist, is an example (see Chapter 6): the editors of the *Neue Bach-Ausgabe* have included both versions in their edition. Similarly, the first edition of the slow movement of Mozart's Sonata in F, K.332 includes many embellishments of repeated material that are absent in the composer's own autograph (Exx. 2.2, 2.3). Most modern editors have chosen to print both versions.[17]

Editors have to deal with a range of issues to do with mistakes, inconsistencies and omissions in sources. Obvious mistakes are easy enough to deal with – they can simply be listed in the critical commentary. Inconsistencies and omissions are more troublesome. For a 'scholarly' edition there is not necessarily any need to reach conclusions about these issues – it might be sufficient simply to include in the editions the details as they are found in the sources, leaving the reader to decide what may have been in the composer's mind. However, for a 'performing' edition the user can reasonably expect the editor to have considered the problems and to have offered some solutions. This is indeed the approach of most editors.

Editorial interventions may be distinguished from the composer's own markings by the use of square brackets, vertical or diagonal slashes through editorial slurs, smaller typefaces, etc. However, not all editors notate their interventions with the same degree of rigour. For example, in the event of a musical motif being articulated differently in two or more places within a movement editors even of scholarly, complete editions not infrequently 'rationalise' the articulation (i.e., make each appearance identical). Typically, only the most general of comments appears in the commentary, and there is no specific indication of editorial intervention in the edition. Such an approach deprives the performer of an opportunity to consider the evidence properly, although with careful scrutiny of all of the available editorial information, editors who have taken this sort of approach can usually be identified.

Increasing numbers of facsimile editions have been published in recent years. They have both advantages and disadvantages.

The obvious advantage of facsimiles is that they allow performers to see the music as its contemporaries saw it. The disadvantage is that performers who use them may not have recourse to all the scholarly apparatus that is available to modern editors. This is more of a problem with some facsimiles than others. Many facsimiles have detailed modern prefaces that outline notational and performance issues and some, such as the volumes of *The London pianoforte school* series,[18] have editorial comments and suggestions written onto the scores themselves. Other facsimiles, however, have little or no modern scholarly comment. This is less of a disadvantage if there is a single, carefully notated source for the work (as is the case with much of the early repertory). But if there are numerous sources of a work, or numerous difficulties with a single source, a facsimile will almost certainly be the second-best option to consulting a good modern edition. Beethoven's piano sonatas illustrate the issues. Facsimiles exist of all of the first editions.[19] However, a modern editor has access to a great deal of research that has been

Ex. 2.4 F. Chopin, Prelude in E major, bars 1–2

undertaken on Beethoven's sketches and autographs as well as the early editions and proof-corrected copies of these works. In addition, Beethoven's pupil Czerny left valuable information on the performance of the works that purports to have originated with the composer.[20] All of these sources will be taken into account by a good modern editor, who will be able to make well-informed suggestions and observations about performance.

Aspects of notation

Staff notation was not always used with the same degree of precision in previous centuries as it is nowadays. This observation applies especially to scores from before the end of the eighteenth century, although it is also true of some aspects of later notation. For example, the modern 'rule' that accidentals apply to all subsequent notes of that pitch within the same bar was not applied so rigidly, so that accidentals are not always cancelled out in early sources. Similarly, composers were not necessarily strict in their notation of rhythmic values. Long notes were not always held for their full value and dotted rhythms were not necessarily played as they were written.

Triplets were often notated as dotted rhythms. A triplet crotchet-plus-quaver rhythm is frequently notated as a dotted quaver followed by a quaver. This practice persisted into the nineteenth century and has been commented upon in the works of several composers. It is an issue, for example, in the performance of Chopin's E major Prelude, where the notated semiquaver in the second beat of the right-hand part of bar 1 is aligned in early sources above the triplet quaver (Ex. 2.4). This notation is consistently followed in the right-hand part until bar 9 of the work, whereas the dotted rhythm of the left-hand part is written differently. A similar notation is found, for example, in some of Schubert's piano works.[21]

Double-dotting and *notes inégales* conventions are further rhythmic

Ex. 2.5 J. S. Bach, Chromatic Fantasia, BWV 903, bars 27–8

Ex. 2.6 J. Haydn, Variation 9 from the Variations Hob.XVII:2, bars 1–2

aspects of performance of which keyboard players need to be aware. They are touched upon in Chapter 6 in relation to Bach's *French Overture*.

Notation is sometimes a shorthand for what is actually played. The practices of embellishment and improvisation at certain 'cues' in early keyboard music scores will be discussed in Chapter 5, but one relatively common shorthand should be mentioned here – the use of terms such as 'arpeggio' in association with sequences of chords that are usually notated in long note values. This occurs, among other places, in the middle of the Fantasia of Bach's Chromatic Fantasia and Fugue, BWV 903 and in some of the preludes and other movements of Handel's suites. Sometimes, the spread of the first chord is fully notated by the composer in order to indicate how the rest of the passages should be arpeggiated (Ex. 2.5). In other examples the keyboard player is free to arpeggiate as he or she wishes – with a simple, upwards spread, with a combination of upwards and downwards spreading, and with or without the addition of acciaccaturas (see Chapter 7).

Many keyboard works before the late eighteenth century have apparently unplayable, wide intervals in left-hand parts (Ex. 2.6). The reason for their existence is straightforward: the lower register of many early keyboard instruments was not fully chromatic, but used instead some form of 'short octave'. Certain pitches were played on keys that looked as if they were made for others. So, for example, in the most common early arrangement of the bass register of the keyboard the lowest note, C, was sounded by playing the key for the note E. D was to be found on the F♯ key, and E on G♯. F was in the usual place and the keyboard became fully chromatic upwards from A. On a minority of instruments the F♯ and G♯ keys were divided so that the back and front of each key played different notes. The front F♯ key played D and the back F♯ key played F♯. Similarly, the front G♯ key played E and back G♯ key played G♯.

As keyboard compass extended, different short octaves came into use. Probably the most complex was that developed in Austria in the eighteenth century.[22] Four split keys are sometimes necessary, with one of them divided to play three different notes.

The music-publishing boom that began towards the end of the eighteenth century and continued into the nineteenth had significant effects on the way in which music notation developed. Whereas earlier music had tended to be written for performance by the composer, or by musicians known to the composer, much late eighteenth- and nineteenth-century music was written specifically for publication, and therefore for performers over whom the composers had no influence. The result was an increasing tendency for composers to include specific performance directions in their works. However, although the general trend was towards more performance detail, the actual amount of it found in works of the period varies enormously.

At one extreme during the period under discussion are those works that contain little or no performance detail. The reason for this is most unlikely to be that the composer had no specific intentions in mind regarding those works' performance. The absence of directions may simply reflect the fact that the composer was short of time. This is true of many of Mozart's concertos (see Chapter 6). Despite the increasing tendency for music to be published during the period, Mozart seldom prepared his concertos for publication – the earliest sources are manuscript.

Performers may not be given many clues about the way in which Mozart intended his concertos to be played, but by studying other works that were much more meticulously marked by the composer it is possible to establish what he considered to be desirable in performance. While Mozart did not always prepare his works very thoroughly for publication, he sometimes included remarkably detailed performance indications, such as those of the Sonata in C minor, K.457, completed in 1784 and published (with the C minor Fantasia, K.475) in the following year. Throughout the work, but especially in the slow movement, details of dynamics are given for each hand

Ex. 2.7 W.A. Mozart, Sonata in C minor, K.457, slow movement, bar 14

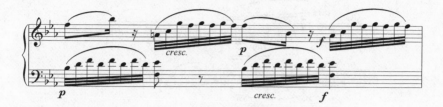

Ex. 2.8 W.A. Mozart, Sonata in C minor, K.457, slow movement, bar 21

Ex. 2.9 W.A. Mozart, Sonata in C minor, K.457, slow movement, bars 22–3

(Ex. 2.7) and some phrases are given the most extraordinary level of dynamic attention (Ex. 2.8). Articulation markings abound, mostly in the right-hand part (Ex. 2.9) and there are several examples of what appears to be written-out *rubato* (Ex. 2.10 – see Chapter 5). When the opening melody returns in bars 17 and 41 it is extensively embellished. There are also small-note flourishes, unusual in sonatas, as well as a short, written-out cadenza towards the end of the movement (bar 52). Such detail is rarely equalled in eighteenth-century scores, but it provides modern performers with an insight into the level of care with which Mozart prepared his own performances.

Nineteenth-century scores are no more consistent in the level of performance detail that they contain than their late eighteenth-century counterparts. The majority of nineteenth-century scores contain few, if any, details of pedalling, rhythmic flexibility, dynamics and articulation. But just occasionally

Ex. 2.10 W.A. Mozart, Sonata in C minor, K.457, slow movement, bar 19

Ex. 2.11 F. Chopin, Etude Op. 25, No. 11, bar 57

a composer marked in a degree of detail that is comparable with Mozart's discussed in the previous paragraph. One such publication is Liszt's *Grandes Etudes* (Fig. 2.2). In this work there is a remarkable level of detail regarding almost every aspect of performance which must surely inform the performance of others of his works with fewer performance directions.

Finally, it is important for a keyboard player to assess the primary purpose of the notation: does it represent the sound that is made, or does it represent what the performer's hands actually do? The two are not necessarily the same. The left-hand part of Example 2.11 is a striking example of notation that indicates what the hand should do, rather than how it sounds. It is necessary for the fifth finger of the performer's left hand to release the low E on the first beat of the bar quickly, in order to change places with the thumb on the E an octave higher during the course of the first beat. This is the reason for the staccato dot under the low E, which will nevertheless sound until the middle of the bar, because of the action of the sustaining pedal. The notation of a staccato dot at the same time as an indication for the sustaining pedal may look peculiar, but in this instance it has a logic that tells the performer precisely what the left hand should do.

Fig. 2.2 F. Liszt, *Grandes Etudes*, No. 2. At the bottom of the page is an explanation of three performance directions: the first indicates the holding up of the tempo to a lesser degree than is normally indicated by a pause while the second and third indicate accelerando and rallentando respectively.

3   The instruments

An essential first step in the preparation of a historically informed performance is the choice of an appropriate instrument. As Chapter 2 pointed out, different repertories were written for different instruments and it is therefore necessary to know where and when instruments were popular. It is also important to know about the resources of those instruments; decisions about registration and pedalling, for example, depend on knowledge of instrument specifications.

Unfortunately, the harpsichords, early pianos and other keyboard instruments now in use do not truly reflect the variety of instruments that existed in earlier centuries. Accidents of history have meant that certain types of instrument have survived and have been copied in large numbers while others are scarcely ever encountered. So, for example, a large proportion of the harpsichords currently in use are copies of early Italian, Ruckers-style, or eighteenth-century French instruments, whereas early German, French and English types, as well as their eighteenth-century Austrian counterparts, are rare. Similarly, there are many reproductions of *c.* 1800 Viennese pianos, but very few copies of early or mid-eighteenth-century types. Nevertheless, with some careful investigation it is possible to become acquainted with the main characteristics of a representative selection of the instruments for which keyboard composers wrote. This chapter provides an overview of the subject, but much more detailed accounts will be found in the literature cited in endnotes and in the Select Bibliography. Recordings can also give an impression of the sound of the instruments. However, there is no substitute for seeing and hearing the instruments 'in the flesh', which it is possible to do by visiting some of the major keyboard instrument collections. Bevan includes details of the major British collections[1] while collections further afield are listed by Boalch.[2]

Harpsichords

A great deal of useful information on the history of the harpsichord, spinet and clavichord will be found in Russell's and Hubbard's
important studies, as well as in the more recent work of Ripin, O'Brien and
others.[3]

Harpsichords were known as early as 1397 and the earliest surviving
plucked-string instrument dates from c. 1480,[4] by which time harpsichords
were known in Italy, Germany, France and England.[5] Only a small number
of sixteenth-century harpsichords survive from Flanders, Germany and
England and they have been fully described by O'Brien and Koster.[6] A larger
number of Italian instruments (about forty) exist from the same period,
many of which have undergone extensive alteration over the centuries – a
factor that has been taken into account only in the most recent histories of
the harpsichord, but which crucially affects registration and some other
matters.[7]

Sixteenth-century Italian harpsichords have a characteristically clear
sound that is a result of their light construction. The case sides, which are
usually of cypress, are very thin (3–6mm) and overlap the baseboard, by
contrast with instruments of the Flemish and other traditions. Italian
instruments were usually placed in a second, decorated case and the whole is
usually referred to as an 'inner–outer' case construction. The shape is typically long and slender with a deeply-curved bentside and it appears that only
single-manual instruments were made. A number of sixteenth-century
Italian harpsichords had a single 8′ register while rather more (and especially those made in Venice) had an 8′ and 4′, the ends of whose jack rails
projected through the cheek of the instrument (the side of the harpsichord
to the right of the performer). Most sixteenth-century Italian instruments
were strung in iron.

Seventeenth-century Italian harpsichords were constructed in much the
same way as their predecessors, although some instruments were made with
a single, thicker case (rather than the earlier inner–outer case structure).
There was also a strong preference for instruments with two 8′ registers,
some of which had been made towards the end of the sixteenth century.
(Many earlier harpsichords with a single 8′ register, or an 8′ and 4′, were
altered during the course of the seventeenth century in order to conform to

more modern requirements.) Some instruments with three 8′ registers were also built. From around the middle of the century a few double-manual harpsichords with two 8′s and one 4′ were made (at least some of which had no coupler and incorporated the 4′ on the upper manual). There is also evidence to suggest that some instruments with a 16′ register were built. On many instruments from this period, and from the eighteenth century, there is no means for changing the registers – sometimes the plectra for both 8′s are fixed in a single jack. Brass stringing seems to have been favoured on seventeenth-century Italian harpsichords, as opposed to the earlier preference for iron.

A number of sixteenth- and seventeenth-century Italian harpsichords, organs and other keyed instruments were made with split keys in order to distinguish enharmonic equivalents. So, for example, A♭ and G♯ often had their own pipes or strings and were tuned differently. The relevant key was divided, leaving the choice of A♭ or G♯ to the performer. A number of seventeenth-century Italian composers wrote music with extreme modulations that were designed to exploit the possibilities of split-keyed instruments. The existence of these instruments and their music underlines the importance given to unequal temperaments at the time (see below) and it is significant that many of them had their split keys removed in the late seventeenth and eighteenth centuries.[8]

Most of the constructional features of seventeenth-century Italian harpsichords are found in their eighteenth-century counterparts. Harpsichords with two 8′ registers were preferred and double-manual instruments continued to be rare. In common with developments elsewhere in Europe, compass increased from around 4½ octaves to 5, FF–f^3, occasionally a tone higher.

Members of the Ruckers family are central to the history of the harpsichord in northern Europe from the sixteenth century onwards.[9] The dynasty began with the work of Hans Ruckers (c. 1550–98) in Antwerp and continued until just after the end of the seventeenth century in the hands of the Couchets, who had married into the Ruckers family. The Ruckers family made a number of different harpsichord models at different pitches, but the design of each changed very little between the closing decades of the sixteenth century and the middle of the seventeenth century. The typical single-manual instrument has an 8′ and 4′ and a compass of C/E to c^3. The two keyboards of the double-manual model cannot be coupled and each manual has an 8′ and 4′. There are just two sets of strings: the 8′ and 4′ registers of each keyboard operate the same set. The compasses of the two keyboards differ: the upper-manual compass is C/E to c^3 while the lower manual is C/E to f^3. The upper-manual keyboard is not aligned with the lower, but begins to the right of it, so that the top notes of each keyboard are placed one above the other; in other words the c^3 of the upper manual sounds at the same pitch as the f^3 of the lower, and so on throughout the compass. A harp (sometimes also referred to as buff) stop, in which small pieces of leather are attached to a movable wooden batten, was customary on Ruckers harpsichords. When the pieces of leather come into contact with the strings, the upper harmonics are damped and the sustaining capability of the string is diminished, producing a plucking effect. Other less common types of Ruckers harpsichords exist, including the combined harpsichord/virginal.

The construction of Ruckers harpsichords was such that the case sides, internal bracing and wrestplank were assembled first, before the baseboard and soundboard were added. The case sides, which sit on top of the baseboard, are made of poplar and are rather thicker than the case sides of their Italian counterparts. The plucking point of the 8′ register is nearer to the player than it is on early Italian instruments, producing a more nasal quality.

Around the middle of the seventeenth century, by which time the family business had passed to the Couchets, some innovations were made. The compass was extended and a disposition of two 8′ registers was used – a disposition that seems to have been very popular all over Europe at the time.

In the eighteenth century members of the Dulcken family were among the most prominent Flemish makers. The most important member of the family was Johann Daniel, who worked in Antwerp. Most of his single- and double-manual harpsichords have a disposition of two 8′s and a 4′. In addition, his double-manual instruments include a lute stop, which operates a separate row of jacks which are closer to the end of the string than the other registers, and which produces a nasal sound.

Very little is known about harpsichord building in France before 1600, largely because the instruments have not survived. Some seventeenth-century harpsichords still exist, especially from the second half of the century, by makers such as Desruisseaux, Richard, Tibaut and Vaudry, but they are less well-documented than their Italian or Flemish counterparts.

Seventeenth-century French harpsichords seem to have been more lightly constructed than the instruments of the Ruckers family, but not so lightly as their Italian counterparts. The most common disposition was evidently two manuals (at the same pitch), each with its own set of 8' strings, and a 4' register, so that music requiring two keyboards (see below, p. 50) could be played. At some point during the century a coupling mechanism was invented. Both brass and iron stringing was used.

A number of double-manual harpsichords with a larger than usual chromatic compass were made by the Ruckers for the French market in the seventeenth century. This fact is particularly significant, since during the eighteenth century some of these instruments underwent a *ravalement* – an alteration – by such important makers as Blanchet and Taskin. Typically, the un-aligned Ruckers keyboards were put into alignment, some extra notes were added, and the disposition altered to two 8's and a 4'.

Around the end of the seventeenth and the beginning of the eighteenth centuries the construction of French harpsichords changed from relatively thin-cased instruments in which the case walls overlap the baseboard to harpsichords built in the Ruckers tradition with thick cases which sit on top of the baseboard. These eighteenth-century harpsichords, by makers such as Blanchet, Donzelague, Goermans, Hemsch and Taskin,[10] are richer and fuller in sound than their seventeenth-century French predecessors and are among the grandest harpsichords ever built. A full 5-octave compass, FF–f³, was used at least as early as 1711 (in an instrument by Donzelague). Two-manual instruments continued to be favoured, with two 8's, a 4' and a coupler. The buff stop, used on Ruckers harpsichords, was not common on French instruments in the first half of the eighteenth century, but was usual thereafter. Another device for modifying the sound of French harpsichords was the *peau de buffle*, used by Taskin from 1768. It consists of a separate row of jacks containing soft leather plectra which produce a quieter sound than the stiffer quills of the other registers.

Little reliable information is available concerning harpsichord-building traditions in sixteenth- and seventeenth-century German-speaking lands. Some aspects of what little is known about them will be mentioned briefly and in passing in the pages that follow. In the eighteenth century, however, there were at least three separate traditions. In Hamburg the Hass and Fleischer families were the most notable harpsichord builders. This tradition seems to have had little to do with that of the Ruckers family. Some of the large instruments of this school have organ-like elements to their dispositions, including three manuals (the only unquestionably genuine three-manual harpsichord in existence was made by Hieronymus Albrecht Hass in 1740). H. A. Hass also made harpsichords with 16' and 2' registers and sometimes included lute (also favoured on earlier German and English instruments) and harp stops. There is also evidence to suggest that Fleischer used 16' registers.[11]

A number of instrument makers flourished in Saxony (Gräbner, Horn and Silbermann) and in Berlin (Mietke). In 1719 Bach took delivery of a two-manual Mietke harpsichord for the Prince of Anhalt-Cöthen.[12] Bach's later association with Silbermann is documented in the section of this chapter that refers to pianos. To judge from the surviving harpsichords these makers constructed their instruments more lightly than the Hamburg school. The most popular type had two manuals with two 8's and a 4' (a lute stop was also quite common and the harp was sometimes used) and the single-manual instruments have two 8's. There is evidence, however, that Mietke made instruments with a 16' register.[13]

An eighteenth-century Viennese tradition of harpsichord building has recently been identified.[14] The instruments of this tradition have a similar appearance to early pianos made in Vienna: their cases are usually of walnut and have sloping cheeks. The case sides are thin and the instruments have one manual and two 8's. A particularly complex short-octave arrangement is a characteristic of Austrian instruments.[15]

Details of early harpsichords made in England are difficult to establish, but it is likely that they shared features of the early German and especially the early Flemish traditions, since a number of Flemish makers are known to have worked in London throughout the sixteenth century.[16] The earliest extant English harpsichord was made by a Flemish maker, Theeuwes, in 1579 and the next surviving instrument was made by an English maker, Hasard, in 1622.[17] It shares many characteristics of early German and Flemish instruments, themselves not dissimilar to harpsichords built in the early Italian tradition. It had a lid, however, and was therefore probably not placed in an outer case. The instrument is a single-manual and evidently had three sets of strings whose pitch remains uncertain. A lute register was included, and there may also have been a buff stop. A later, single-manual harpsichord of 1683 by Charles Haward has two 8's and a lute stop.

A number of foreign makers such as Zenti, Tisseran and Tabel worked in England alongside British makers such as the Hitchcocks in the seventeenth and early eighteenth centuries. By the second quarter of the eighteenth century a fairly standard pattern of harpsichord making had emerged that was typified in the harpsichords of Shudi and Kirkman, pupils of Hermann Tabel, who brought with him the Ruckers tradition from Antwerp. The instruments of Shudi and Kirkman are heavily built and there are three standard models: a single-manual with either two 8's or two 8's and a 4' and a double-manual. The double-manuals are characterised by a fixed upper keyboard whose 8' register can be played on the lower manual by means of a dogleg mechanism. An additional 8' and 4' are customary as well as lute and buff registers. A particular feature of Shudi's instruments after c. 1765 is an additional half-octave in the bass, down to CC, making a total of 5½ octaves.

Apart from the harpsichord-building traditions outlined above, instruments were made in other parts of Europe such as the Iberian peninsula, Switzerland and Scandinavia. These traditions are, as yet, relatively poorly documented.[18]

The concern for more changes in tone colour and dynamics than one would normally associate with the harpsichord can be traced back at least as far as the closing decades of the seventeenth century, particularly in England. Its most extravagant early expression is Thomas Mace's description of a harpsichord by Charles Haward with four registration pedals allowing, as Mace claimed, twenty-four 'varieties' of sound (see Chapter 4).[19] The instrument was unusual, but not unique, at the time.

Registration or 'machine' pedals, which operated the stop mechanisms, became a regular feature of English harpsichords from at least as early as the middle of the 1760s.[20] Similar devices, operated by knee levers, were known in France from the late 1750s onwards and are found most commonly on Taskin's harpsichords.[21] In addition to mechanical devices for quick registration changes there were swell mechanisms which enabled part of the lid, or a number of shutters placed over the strings, to be lowered or raised. Lid swells were used on harpsichords by Backers, Kirkman, Weber and others from the mid 1760s and Shudi patented his 'Venetian swell' mechanism (with shutters directly above the strings) in 1769.[22] All of these inventions were a response to the growing demand for dynamic flexibility that also resulted in the increasing popularity of the piano at the time.

Virginals and spinets

Up-to-date information regarding the history of virginals and spinets will be found in the literature of the harpsichord.

Virginals and spinets are smaller (though not necessarily quieter) plucked-string keyboard instruments that usually have a single set of strings and jacks. The terminology associated with these instruments is somewhat confusing (see Chapter 4 for a fuller discussion). 'Virginals' is a term used generically for a variety of string keyboard instruments (including harpsi-chords) in England well into the seventeenth century. During the same period, 'épinette' was used in France for all plucked-string keyboard instru-ments. 'Virginal' and 'spinet' are sometimes used interchangeably in the case of polygonal plucked-string keyboard instruments. However, 'in the pre-ferred current usage, "spinet" refers to an instrument whose strings run diagonally from left to right with respect to the keyboard',[23] which means that all other instruments in this category, whether rectangular or polygo-nal, are called 'virginals'.

Many aspects of virginal construction follow the national trends of harp-sichord building. Italian virginals typically have very thin case sides which overlap the baseboard and the instruments sit in a more sturdy outer case. Flemish virginals of the sixteenth century and later have thicker cases, the shell of which was assembled before the base was fixed.

Flemish virginals were more popular than the extent of their current use suggests. They were made in substantial numbers by the Ruckers family[24] and varied in size according to pitch. They were made in two standard designs. The so-called muselar virginal has its keyboard to the right of the instrument and the strings are plucked at about one-third of their length. The strings pass over two bridges, both of which lie over an area of freely-vibrating soundboard, and there is an 'arpichordium' stop, by means of which small pieces of metal are made to touch the bass strings, causing a buzzing sound. In the 'spinett virginal' the strings are plucked closer to one end and one of the bridges lies over a solid piece of wood. The sound is more like a harpsichord, rather than the 'flutey' sound of the muselar. A third, much rarer, type was also made in Flanders, with a keyboard situated in the centre of the instrument.

Smaller virginals at 4′ pitch were also made which could sit on top of either a muselar or spinett virginal. The combination of the two is known as 'mother and child' and the mechanisms of the two instruments could be coupled so that a combination of 8′ and 4′ could be achieved, as on a harpsichord.

The nineteen extant British virginals are listed by Boalch[25] and date from the period 1641–84, although both locally made and European virginals are known to have been used in Britain well before then. British virginals are rectangular with keyboards to the left of the instrument. They are similar in construction to Flemish instruments.

The earliest surviving spinets are from the seventeenth century and are Italian in origin. They are small, and are designed to be played an octave above normal pitch. It was possibly an Italian, Zenti, who invented the larger type of bentside spinet that was to be particularly popular in England from the late seventeenth century onwards.

Clavichords

The literature of the clavichord has increased significantly in recent years through the work of Brauchli and others.[26]

The clavichord is different from other early keyboard instruments in that its strings are struck by small metal tangents, thereby making the instrument touch-sensitive. References to clavichords date from the beginning of the fifteenth century, and during the first part of the instrument's history it was evidently popular across continental Europe and in Britain. By the seventeenth century the clavichord had become much less common, but was still not totally unknown, in Italy, England and France. It remained popular, however, in Germany, Austria, Scandinavia and Iberia. Of the surviving instruments, most are of German origin and the contemporary literature shows that it was particularly popular there. Seventeenth-century (and later) clavichords are characterised by the fact that the keyboard is built inside the case, rather than protruding from it, as in earlier instruments. Although in the seventeenth century almost all clavichords were fretted (the small metal tangents of more than one note act upon a single pair of strings) there was a tendency for fewer notes to be played on the same string than had previously been the case; two notes per pair of strings became more usual, while the bass of the instrument was unfretted. The first reference to a completely unfretted clavichord is dated 1693.[27]

A few clavichords and some references to them survive from eighteenth-century Italy, England and France, but most activity concerning the clavichord in the eighteenth century was in Scandinavia, Germany and some of its bordering countries as well as the Iberian peninsula. While many eighteenth-century clavichords were fretted (most of the eighteenth-century repertory can be played on such instruments), a number of makers began to make much larger, unfretted instruments, some with a compass exceeding five octaves. In an attempt to increase the power of the bass extra 4′ strings were sometimes used. This feature is found in the clavichords of H. A. and J. A. Hass in Hamburg, but not in instruments by other prominent makers of the same period, such as Friederici and Hubert. Throughout the clavichord's history makers added pedals to clavichords, chiefly, it seems, to enable organists to practise.

The clavichord's popularity outlived that of the plucked-string keyboard instruments. Inevitably, fewer instruments were made in the nineteenth century, although examples from as late as the 1840s exist. Some particularly large nineteenth-century instruments, with 5½ or even 6 octaves, were made in Sweden by Wessberg and Nordqvist.

Pianos

The modern literature of the piano is extensive. Since the important studies of Harding and Ehrlich,[28] the history of the eighteenth-century piano has received particularly close attention, especially in the work of Pollens, Cole and Maunder.[29] A number of less detailed overviews of the subject have also been published.[30]

The earliest pianos were made in, or just before, the year 1700 by Bartolomeo Cristofori in Florence. Three complete grand pianos by Cristofori survive as well as the keyboard and action of a fourth.[31] In external appearance these pianos resemble harpsichords and the compass is modest – 4 or 4½ octaves. The action is sophisticated and very light to play. In two of the surviving pianos the hammers are made only of rolled and glued parchment covered with leather.

Cristofori's pianos did not enjoy immediate, unqualified success. Although they were apparently used for solo performance as well as for accompanying, early commentators such as Maffei, who published a description of the new invention in 1711, found the instrument's touch-sensitive action difficult to control.[32] Some other aspects of the piano were also compared unfavourably with the harpsichord, which at that time had a more powerful tone.

Despite the early piano's shortcomings, news of it spread and instruments based on Cristofori's design were made by a variety of makers. Maffei's description was translated and published in Mattheson's *Critica musica* (Hamburg, 1725). Five Florentine pianos, presumably by Cristofori or his pupil Ferrini,[33] were purchased by Maria Barbara of Spain, perhaps at the instigation of Domenico Scarlatti[34] and a mid-eighteenth-century Iberian piano-making tradition was based on Cristofori's design.[35] At least two pianos were known in London in the first half of the eighteenth century. Charles Burney relates how Samuel Crisp brought a piano back from Rome which he had probably purchased in the late 1730s, and which was later copied by the London maker Plenius.[36] Another piano of Italian origin was known in Handel's circle.[37]

In Germany, Christoph Gottlieb Schröter claimed to have invented a hammer action in 1717, but whether he ever made a complete instrument is not known.[38] Of greater significance, however, is the work of Gottfried Silbermann. J. S. Bach was at first critical of his pianos, but later praised them.[39] Silbermann first made pianos as early as the beginning of the 1730s, but his three surviving grands date from the late 1740s. Although aspects of the case design of Silbermann's pianos resemble contemporary German harpsichords, the actions and some other aspects of their design are close copies of Cristofori's, suggesting that the German maker had seen some of the Italian's instruments. There are differences, however, for example in the stops found on the instruments of each maker (see Chapter 4).

A type of piano design very similar to that of Gottfried Silbermann is found in the instruments of his nephew, Johann Heinrich, who worked in Strasbourg. Apart from some earlier experiments by Marius and Weltman,[40] Silbermann's pianos were probably the earliest in Paris. A newspaper advertisement in 1759 describes a piano that resembles the work of that maker, and in 1761 another advertisement stated that four J. H. Silbermann pianos were in Paris. The organist Daquin owned a J. H. Silbermann piano in 1769. Two of J. H. Silbermann's instruments survive, both dating from the 1770s.[41] Some French makers followed the Cristofori–Silbermann tradition: a grand piano by Louis Bas, made near Avignon in 1781, shares many features of the

Silbermann instruments (action design, inverted wrestplank, etc.) and it has been suggested that Blanchet's pianos of the 1760s were made similarly.[42]

While a number of individuals were producing horizontal grand pianos in the Cristofori–Silbermann tradition, other types of keyboard instruments were also being made. Before the middle of the century, 'pyramids', or vertical grand pianos, started to be made – tall, hammer-action keyboard instruments that look like up-ended grands, except that they are symmetrical, coming to a point in the middle at the top of the instrument.[43] Also around the middle of the eighteenth century, Christian Ernst Friederici is credited with the invention of the square piano in Germany. Whether or not this was so, a number of small, domestic instruments survive in this form from the second half of the century.[44]

A close relative of the piano, the pantalon, was popular from the middle of the eighteenth century.[45] The instrument was named after Pantaleon Hebenstreit, a renowned performer on an enlarged dulcimer with no dampers that he played with hand-held, wooden or cloth-covered beaters. Keyed pantalons were mostly similar in shape to square pianos. They typically had wooden hammers and a variety of means for varying the sound, many of which were incorporated into piano design. One of the most usual stops found on pantalons was the so-called moderator, a device that interposed a strip of cloth between the hammers and strings – a stop that is frequently found on 'Viennese' pianos (see below). A harp stop was often included too, as well as a mechanism for lowering the dampers onto the strings, similar to the device found on many eighteenth-century pianos, beginning with Silbermann (see Chapter 4).

Another kind of keyboard instrument in which the strings are struck by a hard object is the *Tangentenflügel*, whose sound-producing mechanism is a bare wooden jack that is thrown against the strings.[46] Späth and Schmahl made many such instruments in the closing decades of the eighteenth century. They resemble contemporary Viennese grands in appearance and, like the pantalon, have an array of stops.

During the eighteenth century combination keyboard instruments reached a peak of popularity. The idea of uniting two types of instrument was not new – organ/harpsichord combinations had been known for centuries. However, at a time when there was little agreement about the merits of one type of instrument over another it was perhaps inevitable that combination piano/harpsichords and piano/organs should be relatively common. The earliest-known piano/harpsichord is a double-manual instrument by the Italian maker Ferrini dated 1746.[47] There were numerous others, including an instrument brought from Hamburg to England by William Mason in 1755 and instruments by Merlin and Stodart as well as an instrument of related design by Stein.[48] A number of piano/organs also survive from this period.

As the preceding paragraphs show, the mid-eighteenth century (during which Mozart grew up and in which Haydn and his contemporaries wrote many of their keyboard works) was a period of great invention when numerous different sorts of touch-sensitive keyboard instruments existed alongside one another. However, very few copies exist of any of the pianos and other instruments mentioned so far in this section, so that their sound is as yet largely unfamiliar to modern audiences.

Apart from the few, isolated examples of the piano in London in the middle of the eighteenth century, the history of the English grand piano begins with the work of Americus Backers.[49] Backers almost certainly began to make grand pianos in the late 1760s. His single surviving piano, dated 1772 and now in the Russell Collection, Edinburgh, resembles an English harpsichord of the period in external appearance, but has an action which is based on Cristofori's design and which is light, but not quite as responsive as the Viennese action (see below). There are two pedals, an *una corda* and a sustaining pedal (the same two pedals found on almost all English grands). Backers' design forms the basis for all English grand pianos to the middle of the nineteenth century. He died in 1778 but his work was continued at first by Robert Stodart, then by John Broadwood (whose first recorded grand was made in 1785) and then by a host of other makers. The distinctive English action designed by Backers and refined by other makers[50] forms the basis of the modern grand piano.

The developments that took place in the design of the English grand are far too numerous to mention here. However, it is important for the performer of late eighteenth- and early nineteenth-century music to realise that these changes took place very rapidly, and that the instruments of one decade are substantially different from those of another. One of the most significant developments was the extension of the piano's compass. Until the end of the 1780s, 5 octaves, from FF to f^3, was normal, but in 1790

Broadwood extended the compass to 5½ octaves (FF–c^4) and then, probably in 1794, to 6 octaves (CC–c^4).[51] (Other makers in London also extended the compass in the 1790s, some to 6 octaves, FF–f^4.) Compass was extended again in the early nineteenth century to 6½ octaves and then more gradually to that in use today.

As the keyboard was extended the piano grew in other ways too. Heavier strings and greater string tension meant that larger hammers, and therefore a deeper touch, were required. The greater total string tension meant that the piano needed strengthening and shortly after the beginning of the nineteenth century pieces of metal began to be used in the more vulnerable parts of the frame. All these developments meant that an English grand piano of, say, 1830 requires a very different technique from the first Backers instruments.

The earliest English square piano was made in 1766[52] by Johann Zumpe, one of a number of northern European instrument makers and musicians who settled in London in the middle of the eighteenth century. Zumpe quickly developed a market for these compact and inexpensive domestic instruments. J. C. Bach published music for the new instrument in the same year and Zumpe's square pianos quickly became fashionable; so fashionable that Zumpe could not keep pace with the demand. Other makers such as Pohlman and Beyer quickly stepped in to supply the market, basing their instruments on Zumpe's design, although from the 1780s onwards Geib and others modified the action in order to make it capable of more subtle playing. From the end of the eighteenth century and into the nineteenth the developments in compass and mechanism that took place in the English grand were paralleled in the square. Details of the stops and pedals found on English squares are given in Chapter 4.

In France, J. H. Silbermann's pianos and instruments based on the same design were used in the 1760s and later. However, from around 1770 the French market was flooded by English imports, especially of square pianos. The extent to which this was so can be seen by the fact that the majority of pianos owned by the French nobility at the time of the Revolution were made by Zumpe, his successor Schoene and other London makers including Pohlman and Beck.[53] Early French makers such as Mercken and Erard followed the English design of squares.

A few French grands with a design unlike Silbermann's or English grands were made by Taskin,[54] but French grand piano manufacture gained in impetus when Sebastien Erard returned to Paris from working with Broadwood in London in *c*. 1794. Erard (whose pianos were later favoured by Liszt) used the model of the English grand as the basis for his work, and many of the developments that subsequently took place in France were similar to those in England (with the exception of the pedals that were preferred in the early nineteenth century – see Chapter 4). Probably Erard's best-known contribution to the development of the instrument was the invention, in 1822, of the repetition action, which facilitated the repetition of notes without the necessity of the keys being fully released – a necessary development, considering the depth of touch of Erard's pianos. The repetition action was not adopted by all French makers, however. Pleyel's pianos, which were preferred by Chopin, were lighter to play and did not have the depth of touch of Erard's, and therefore had no need of a complex repetition action.

A variety of types of grand piano existed in Germany and Austria in the late eighteenth century,[55] but undoubtedly the most influential maker of the period was J. A. Stein of Augsburg, whose many pupils worked throughout southern Germany and Austria. From the 1780s he made grand pianos with the distinctive 'Viennese' action. Stein's version of the 'Viennese' action differs in some details from the type of action made by other makers such as Anton Walter (whose pianos were played by Mozart and Beethoven). However, all versions of the action are fundamentally different from the 'English' action in both appearance and in feel to the performer. The 'Viennese' action is highly sensitive and capable of tiny nuances of articulation, whereas the sense of direct contact with the strings is not so great in the English action. (In the literature of the early nineteenth century the Viennese action is often noted for its 'lightness' as opposed to the 'heaviness' of the English action.)

Stein's business was carried on in Vienna after his death by his daughter, Nannette Streicher. Both she and other makers continued to use the 'Viennese' action for some time, but as the nineteenth century wore on it gradually gave way to the 'English' action. Even so, the 'Viennese' action was still being made by a few makers into the twentieth century.

As in England and France, the compass of 'Viennese' pianos extended quickly around the turn of the century from 5 octaves, eventually to the compass in use today.[56] The instruments grew in size and the string tension increased. Nevertheless, the use of metal was resisted longer by makers of 'Viennese' pianos than it was in England and France.

Like their French counterparts, makers of 'Viennese' pianos in the early decades of the nineteenth century incorporated a greater variety of knee levers and pedals into their instruments than was usual in England. These levers and pedals are described in Chapter 4.

Temperaments

Historical temperaments are discussed in a substantial literature of varying accessibility.[57] The reason for the existence of different temperaments relates to a problem concerning the characteristics of musical intervals and their relationship to each other. For example, if a complete cycle of perfect fifths is tuned, the final note will be not be the same as the first and if three perfect major thirds are tuned the highest note will be slightly less than a perfect octave above the first. While many instrumentalists and singers can adjust individual notes in performance to take account of these peculiarities, keyboard instrument tuners have to adopt systems in which the intervals are tempered.

There is a consensus among writers on the subject that some sort of meantone temperament is appropriate for most keyboard music of the seventeenth century. The main characteristic of meantone tunings is that the major thirds most frequently used are similar in width, as are the two intervals of a tone that make up each of these thirds. In order to achieve this characteristic, most of the fifths are uniformly narrowed. However, this system of tuning causes two main problems. First, the flat/sharp keys (usually f♯, c♯, g♯, b♭ and e♭) cannot be used to play their enharmonic equivalents (g♭, d♭, a♭, a♯ and d♯), because the four major thirds involving these equivalents (g♭–b♭/f♯–a♯, d♭–f, a♭–c, and b–d♯) are far too out of tune. Secondly, the interval of a fifth between (usually) g♯/a♭ and d♯/e♭ is so out of tune as to be completely unusable.

The precise extent to which the fifths were altered in meantone tunings varied and it is difficult to know which type of meantone temperaments were preferred in the seventeenth century. In one popular type of meantone temperament the major thirds most commonly used are perfect (the so-called quarter-comma meantone tuning).

Much of the music of the seventeenth century avoids the problematic intervals of meantone temperaments. However, it was not always necessary for composers to do so since many instruments existed all over Europe in the period with split keys for g♯/a♭ and d♯/e♭. The earliest references to instruments of this sort are in Italian sources (see above), but the practice was common, and existed well into the eighteenth century, further north in Europe (though not so much in France).[58]

Towards the end of the seventeenth century and into the eighteenth, temperaments began to be used that enabled music to be played in all keys, including those using the intervals that had effectively been prohibited by meantone tunings. These newer tunings were sometimes referred to as 'well-tempered' tunings, because of their greater flexibility. The main characteristic of these tunings is that the width of particular intervals within each temperament varies so that, for example, some of the fifths are perfect while the others are tempered, often to varying degrees. Because of the non-uniformity of these temperaments, each key has its own characteristic.

Many theorists devised different well-tempered tunings and some proposed more than one. Among the best-known are those by Werckmeister, Silbermann, Rameau, Kirnberger and Vallotti – there are many others. Werckmeister's preferred tuning is among the least subtle of these; eight of the fifths are perfect while the remaining fifths are tempered similarly to one another. It is generally acknowledged that this tuning suits much music written around 1700, but that its lack of subtlety makes it less useful for later music. Vallotti's tuning contained six perfect fifths, with the other fifths similarly tempered, while other early eighteenth-century figures advocated different degrees of tempering among the imperfect fifths. A number of mid-eighteenth-century musicians considered these more subtle tunings better than Werckmeister's earlier, relatively unrefined well-tempered tuning.[59] It is likely that Bach's '48' were written for a well-tempered tuning of this more sophisticated kind – Lindley has argued that Bach followed no theorist in particular, but favoured the sort of tunings put forward by Sorge and Neidhardt.[60]

Although equal temperament – in which all the semitones are of equal width – was described in sources during the seventeenth and eighteenth centuries, it is doubtful that it had much widespread use before the nineteenth century (some would argue later still[61]). Inevitably, as music became more chromatic and keys with more accidentals became more frequently used, very subtle well-tempered tunings, close to equal temperament, were used in the late eighteenth and early nineteenth centuries.

Purchase, care and tuning of reproduction instruments

It would be invidious to recommend individual makers of reproduction instruments, and somewhat unwise, since new makers quickly come to the fore in what is still essentially a cottage industry. However, anyone who wishes to purchase a new instrument should do their homework by looking out for advertisements in the early music press and by visiting events such as the London Exhibition of Early Music.[62] Second-hand instruments are also in plentiful supply. Advertisements will be found in the early music press and significant displays will be found at, for example, The Early Music Shop in Bradford and The Early Keyboard Agency in Oxford.

Both new and second-hand keyboard instruments are of very varying quality and it is important to find out how any individual instrument responds to changes in environment, if possible, before purchase. An instrument that is in tune and plays well in the showroom may turn out not to keep its tuning, or to have an unreliable action, when it is transported or kept in a different environment.

Since the structures of early keyboard instruments are wooden, they are particularly vulnerable to changes in humidity and the best environment for any keyboard instrument will be one in which the humidity does not vary too much, and which is neither very dry nor very wet. Various factors affect humidity, including the weather, and the location and characteristics of the building in which an instrument is housed (suspended/solid flooring, central heating, etc.), but the conditions can be monitored very easily and inexpensively with a hygrometer. Changing the humidity of a room is more difficult: depending on the size of the room, it is usually only possible to increase the humidity significantly with a humidifier, which can be costly.

Early keyboard instruments do not hold their tuning for long. If humidity changes, the wood expands or contracts and the strings consequently tighten or slacken. The strings will also be affected by changes of temperature, even during the course of a performance (especially under stage lighting). If an instrument is moved it will usually take an hour or more for it to adapt to its new surroundings, so that it is normally best to wait for a while before re-tuning.

Some individuals prefer to tune by ear from a tuning fork (in which case the advice found in some of the practical guides to tuning can be very helpful – see p. 130, note 57), while others use one of the number of tuning meters that are available. The cheaper meters only sound in equal temperament, although with a careful use of their visual displays it is possible to tune other temperaments with their assistance.[63] Expensive tuning meters will enable a variety of different temperaments to be set with ease. When tuning individual strings it is usually best to slacken the string slightly before winding it up to its proper pitch.

Many other problems of early keyboard maintenance, particularly to do with the action, can be easily solved by someone other than a professional, and since broken plectra or strings, sticking jacks, etc., are a relatively frequent occurrence it is best to be prepared to do the job yourself. However, it is possible to damage the delicate actions of early keyboard instruments quite easily, so advice from somebody more experienced is usually the wisest course of action before anything is attempted.

4   Use of instruments and technique

Which instrument?

Deciding which instrument is the most appropriate for any part of the early keyboard repertory can be problematic. The scores of many keyboard pieces contain no mention of any particular instrument while others are labelled ambiguously. Even those that are specific may be difficult to interpret ('for harpsichord or piano', etc.). A number of factors need to be taken into account before a decision is made.

The meaning of some terms associated with the keyboard repertory changed during the period of their use.[1] In 1619 Praetorius commented that the English term 'virginals' referred to a wide variety of plucked-string keyboard instruments.[2] This broad meaning for the term was common throughout the sixteenth and the first half of the seventeenth centuries.[3] It is almost certainly the sense in which the term is used, for example, in *Parthenia or the maydenhead of the first musicke that ever was printed for the virginalls composed by three famous masters: William Byrd, Dr. John Bull & Orlando Gibbons* (1612). From the middle of the seventeenth century, however, formulations such as 'for the virginals or harpsichord' are given, suggesting that the wider use of the term 'virginals' was declining. Moreover, there is some evidence to suggest that the term 'harpsichord' was beginning to be used as the new generic term for plucked-string keyboards in England,[4] although it was frequently used in a more specific sense.

Comparable generic terms were used on the continent. 'Clavicymbal' was used in Flanders throughout the sixteenth, seventeenth and eighteenth centuries to mean any plucked-string keyboard instrument.[5] 'Épinette' was used in France until well into the seventeenth century in much the same way.[6] However, despite the fact that many 'épinettes' were still in use in the eighteenth century, the term never occurs on the title pages of French keyboard music published in the period. The German term 'Clavier' simply meant 'keyboard' or 'keyboard instrument' until the second half of the eighteenth century (though at different times in different places), when it came to be used more specifically for the clavichord.[7] The use of the term 'Flügel' in the eighteenth century has caused some debate – the most persuasive argument is that it generally refers to the harpsichord.[8]

In modern times, the term 'fortepiano' has come to be used to distinguish early instruments from their modern counterparts, usually referred to as 'pianos' or 'pianofortes', although in the eighteenth and early nineteenth centuries 'fortepiano' was just one of a number of terms used to refer to the piano, including 'pianoforte' and 'Hammerklavier'.

Sources of early keyboard music often mention two or more instruments as suitable vehicles for performance. This is especially so in those works which were prepared for publication, for which the publishers and composers wished to attract the largest possible market. Works were published, for example, for 'harpsichord, virginal, or spinet', 'harpsichord, organ, or pianoforte', 'harpsichord, clavichord, or pianoforte', etc. But do such designations imply that the composer had no preference? This is an extremely vexed question. For works such as *Musick's hand-made presenting new and pleasant lessons for the virginals or harpsycon* published by Playford in 1663 and containing works by a variety of composers, we simply do not have sufficient evidence to decide whether the harpsichord or virginals should be preferred. In any case, the difference in timbre between the two instruments is not radically different, so that the alternatives seem equally plausible. For works such as Beethoven's Op. 27 sonatas, however, published in 1802 for 'il clavicembalo o pianoforte', the suggestion that the music is satisfactorily performed on either instrument is implausible: the composer had almost certainly stopped playing the harpsichord some years previously and the work contains specific markings for the piano's damper-raising device. The designation on the title page must surely have been the publisher's way of maximising sales rather than an indication that the composer himself was equally content with performances of the sonatas on either harpsichord or piano.

Beethoven's Op. 27 is an extreme case. For music composed a few decades earlier it is often much more difficult to decide which instrument the composer had in mind, because performers of the period were used to changing from one instrument to another, depending on which was available. So, for example, almost all of Clementi's recorded public performances were on the harpsichord during his early years in London (in the late 1770s), yet his publications in the same period include both piano and harpsichord on their covers.[9] Mozart is a particularly difficult case. It seems that some of his earlier works, such as the concertos K.175, K.238, K.242 and K.246 and some of the variations, were composed for the harpsichord whereas other works were written with the piano in mind. However, he purchased his own piano in the early 1780s, so that his mature keyboard works may be regarded as piano music. Even so, it is known that he continued to play on the clavichord until shortly before his death.[10]

The original function and performance context of a work sometimes suggest that one instrument is more appropriate than another, although it is important to resist conclusions based on modern assumptions. For example, it might be presumed that keyboard music based on sacred melodies is more suited to the organ whereas works based on secular themes are more appropriately performed on stringed keyboard instruments. However, sacred music was often performed in the home – keyboard intabulations and arrangements of choral works along with pieces based on plainsong themes are found in domestic collections alongside dances and works based on popular songs. Furthermore, domestic keyboard music was played on a variety of instruments, including the organ: chamber organs were commonly found in private homes in some countries. Church organs were not always used exclusively for sacred music in liturgical contexts. In parts of post-Reformation northern Europe the organ was more likely to be heard in a concert than in a church context.[11] A mixture of music on sacred and secular themes was probably played on many of these occasions. Even in those parts of Europe where the organ played a significant role in the liturgy, the repertory was not necessarily restricted to works based on sacred themes.

Keyboard idiom can also be a defining factor in deciding which music is better suited to one instrument rather than another. The presence of pedal parts in most cases indicates the organ, although the same repertory might have been practised on stringed keyboard instruments with pedal boards.[12] Much of the French organ repertory was written with the particular colours of the instrument in mind, although some was evidently played on the harpsichord as well, as Gustafson notes:

In general, French organ music, unlike that from other countries, is very different from harpsichord music. Organ textures were determined by characteristic registrations and no one could possibly consider a *tierce-en-taille* as harpsichord music, for example, or an unmeasured prelude as organ music. However, some genres, such as measured preludes and certain noëls, are less idiomatic, and were probably played on either instrument.[13]

Gustafson's remarks on the performance of noëls relates to comments by Michel Corrette in the preface to his *Nouveau livre de noëls* (1753–4), published for harpsichord or organ.

Among stringed keyboard instruments there are differences of capability that are sometimes reflected in performance directions. Dynamic markings usually suggest a piano or clavichord, although some eighteenth-century harpsichord music has graded dynamics such as *crescendo* markings (late eighteenth-century double-manual harpsichords equipped with knee levers or pedals are capable of a surprising range of effects). However, nothing but a clavichord or piano will be able to realise the subtle differences in dynamics between the hands demanded in some scores by Mozart (see Chapter 2). Sustaining pedal effects will only be achievable on the piano.

Although there may be reasons for preferring one instrument to another, the overriding impression of the performance practices of keyboard performers in earlier centuries is one of flexibility: they played on a number of different instruments and changed from one to another with ease.

Harpsichord registration

Compared with the wealth of source material concerning organ registration, there is very little that relates to the harpsichord, either in early treatises and compositions, or in modern texts. The subject is discussed in passing in some of the harpsichord literature,[14] but detailed treatment of the historical evidence is largely confined to the instructions found in eighteenth-century French harpsichord music.[15] In the absence of documentary evidence, an understanding of the instruments' capabilities is all the more crucial (see Chapter 3).

Throughout the period in which music was played on plucked-string instruments keyboard players must have been used to the sound of a single

8′ register, which is adequate for much of the repertory. Some early Italian harpsichords had only one such register, as did the majority of virginals and spinets. However, from early on in the harpsichord's history instruments with two or more registers were made, although on many harpsichords (particularly Italian and Flemish) the performer has to move his or her right hand from the keyboard to the outside of the instrument in order to control the registers. Such changes can only be made when the right hand ceases to play for a few seconds or more, and can therefore only usually be made between movements.

O'Brien has pointed out that the capability of removing the 8′ register on instruments with a single 8′ and 4′ means that the performance of movements on the 4′ register alone is a possibility – one that is generally overlooked by modern performers.[16] This kind of performance may have been common, especially among earlier keyboard players, some of whom would have played harpsichords or spinets equipped only with 4′ registers (i.e., with no 8′).

From around the end of the sixteenth and beginning of the seventeenth century the Italians showed a marked preference for single-manual harpsichords with two 8′s. A similar shift in taste with respect to single-manual instruments can also be seen, though somewhat later, in northern Europe. This strongly suggests a general decline in popularity of the 4′, and the fact that on some instruments it was not possible to separate the two 8′ registers indicates that the two-8′ sound may be considered a standard registration of the period.

Precisely how the lute was used remains a mystery, but considering its prevalence on instruments in Germany, England and elsewhere, we must assume that performers enjoyed its particular colour. Indeed, on English instruments, where there is no coupler, the only way of playing with contrasting 8′ sounds is to use the lute.

The arpichordium stop found on some harpsichords and virginals operated only in the lower part of the instrument, to f^1 (like the piano's bassoon lever or pedal – see p. 53 below), so that a difference in timbre can be effected between the parts of two hands.

The buff stop was confusingly referred to as the 'Laute' in Germany and the 'jeu de luth' in France. It was not used in Italy (where performers seem to have had least interest in contrasting tone-colours) but is found widely in harpsichords elsewhere. Like the arpichordium, the buff was divided in Ruckers' instruments (but not generally elsewhere) so that the timbre of treble and bass could be differentiated. Little is known about the use of the buff stop, but as with the lute, its prevalence suggests that its effect was popular.

In the quest for greater variety of sound in the harpsichord, various means were developed for changing registration more easily. In most harpsichords before the end of the seventeenth century in which the registration was not fixed, the performer made changes by reaching outside of the body of the harpsichord to operate the ends of the registers, which protruded through the side of the instrument. In England, however, developments that facilitated quicker changes of registration occurred at an early date. Stop knobs or levers inside the instrument, near to the keyboard, seem to have been incorporated into some early English harpsichords[17] and in the mid seventeenth century a mechanism for changing registration by means of pedals was developed. The 'pedal' is referred to in a number of English sources in the 1660s and 1670s.[18] It was described in detail by Thomas Mace in 1676:

> *This Instrument* is in *Shape and Bulk* just like a *Harpsicon*; only it differs in the *Order* of *It*, Thus, *viz.* There is made right underneath the *Keys*, near the *Ground*, a kind of *Cubbord*, or *Box* . . . in which . . . the *Performer* sets *both his Feet*, resting them upon his *Heels*, (his *Toes* a little turning up) touching nothing, till such time as he has a *Pleasure* to employ them; which is after this manner, *viz.* There being right underneath his *Toes 4 little Pummels of Wood*, under *each Foot 2*, any one of *Those* 4 he may *Tread* upon at his *Pleasure*; which by the *Weight of his Foot drives a Spring*, and so *Causeth the whole Instrument to Sound*, either *Soft* or *Loud*, according as he shall chuse to Tread any of them down . . .[19]

A number of these instruments were made and instructions for the use of the 'pedal' can be found in a fantasia for violin, bass viol and 'a Pedall Harpsichord or Organ'.[20]

Although the 'pedall' appears to have been something of a rarity at the time, the growing concern for greater tonal variety on the harpsichord is evident in the increasing number of references to instruments with an abundance of registers. *The Daily Courant* for 19 January 1713, for example, advertised a foreign harpsichord and made much of its 'six registers' and its ability to play 'fifty different sounds'.[21] The registral possibilities of continental European harpsichords was indeed increasing by this time (especially in the north), and stop knobs projecting through the nameboard had been introduced in order to facilitate quicker changes. Quirinus von Blankenburg describes how he had rebuilt a Ruckers harpsichord in 1708: 'in order to surprise the listener more quickly through unexpected changes, we brought the stops to the front, so as to be able to move them while playing with a touch of the hand'.[22]

In spite of the evident enthusiasm for tonal variety in the early eighteenth century very few registration indications exist in harpsichord music. Bach's harpsichord registration markings occur mainly in his music that was published during his lifetime. He stipulated performance on two manuals for several numbers of the 'Goldberg Variations', although he never indicates a change of registration in the course of a variation. He also included markings in works such as the *Italian Concerto* and *French Overture* which give us some significant clues as to Bach's registration practice more generally. In these works 'p' and 'f' stipulate changes from one manual to another, but there are no indications for the registration to be changed during the course of a movement. Furthermore, the manual changes occur at important structural moments, especially in the ritornello movements, or in places where an echo is intended: there are no instances where a change is made simply for colouristic purposes.

Instructions for the use of two manuals exist in five works by Handel: the Airs in G minor and B♭ (HWV 466 and 470), the Chaconne in F (HWV 485), the Sonata in G (HWV 579) and the composer's arrangement of the overture from *Amadigi*. Like Bach, Handel uses the two manuals for echo effects and to distinguish the music of each hand in two-part contrapuntal writing.

Registration was used to more expressive ends in the middle of the eighteenth century. In 1747 C. P. E. Bach wrote his *Sonata per il cembalo a 2 tastature* (Wq 69), which has copious dynamic markings for performance on a two-manual instrument. Here, the markings indicate a phrase-by-phrase change in sound (Ex. 4.1) and the directions at the beginnings of movements, or variations, suggest some inventive (if curiously expressed) combinations. The first movement is headed 'forte on the lower manual with all

Ex. 4.1 C. P. E. Bach, *Sonata per il cembalo a 2 tastature* (Wq 69), first movement, bars 1–10

registers, piano on the upper manual' ('Das forte unten mit allen Registern, das piano oben'). The second is headed 'forte with octave and cornet [lute?] on the lower manual, piano on the upper manual' ('Das forte mit Octav und Cornet unten, das piano oben'). For the third movement, a set of variations, a different combination is specified for the theme and each of the nine variations.[23]

The French *clavecinistes* exploited to the full the colouristic possibilities of their harpsichords. Early examples of writing for two manuals can be found in the *pièces croisées* (works in which the music played by the hands crosses in such a way as to be viable only on a two-manual instrument) by Louis Couperin. The works date from the middle of the seventeenth century and demonstrate that French keyboard players of the time must have had access to instruments in which the two keyboards were at the same pitch and on which the registers of the two manuals could be operated independently. We can therefore deduce something about the resources available to the composer, even if further information about registration is not forthcoming.

Eighteenth-century French treatises on harpsichord playing are strangely silent on the question of registration – for example, neither François Couperin nor Saint-Lambert says anything except that weak voices may be accompanied on the upper manual.[24] However, a number of publications by composers in the first half of the century such as F. Couperin, Dandrieu,

Rameau, Dagincourt, Boismortier, Royer and Forqueray include indications for registration.[25] The earliest is found in François Couperin's *Second Livre*. Loosely translated, the instruction for *Les Bagatelles* of the *10ᵉ Ordre* reads 'to play this piece release the coupler, take off the 4′, place the right hand on the upper manual and the left on the lower' ('Pour toucher cette pièce, il faut repousser un des Claviers du Clavecin, ôter la petite octave, poser la main droite sur le Clavier d'en haut, et poser la gauche sur celui d'en bas'). The implication of this, and of other sources, is that the harpsichord would normally be played with the coupler and 4′ engaged.

For *Les Bagatelles* from his *18ᵉ Ordre* (another *pièce croisée*) Couperin offers an alternative mode of performance on a single-manual instrument in which the left hand plays an octave lower than written (or the right hand an octave higher if the left-hand part is too low).

Some of the most detailed instructions for registration are found in Dandrieu's *Premier Livre* (1724):

> *Le Concert des Oiseaux* should be played with both hands on the
> main manual, but with the two unisons taken off, leaving only the 4′;
> *Le Timpanon* requires only the 4′ to be left [on the lower manual],
> but that the right hand plays on the upper manual and the left
> hand on the lower;
> For *les Fifres*, on the contrary, the left hand should be on the upper
> manual and the right on the lower, with just the 4′.

Other works of the period contain less specific instructions, equivalent to the 'p' and 'f' of J. S. Bach's works, including 'p' repetitions of final phrases for a *petite reprise*. It seems that most pieces, however, were intended to be played on one manual, without any contrasting dynamic or colour.

As well as providing the most detailed instructions for harpsichord registration in the first half of the eighteenth century, it was French composers who included markings for the expressive effects made possible by means of knee levers (the equivalent of pedals on English instruments) in the third quarter of the century. Jean-François Tapray specified detailed dynamics in the harpsichord parts of his *Symphonies Concertantes* Op. 8 (1778 – with only a few markings), Op. 9 (1778), Op. 13 (1781), and Op. 15 (1783).[26] The dynamics include *pp, p, f, ff, fp, poco f* and hairpin *crescendo* and *diminuendo* marks, mostly at the beginnings of phrases, although single bars with more than one marking also occur. In Tapray's later *Deux Symphonies pour le clavecin*, Op. 21 (1784) markings for the *peau de buffle* are also found. Even more detailed markings (including dynamics, manual changes and registration) are found in Armand-Louis Couperin's *Simphonie*, dating probably from the 1770s. The work survives only in manuscript, but a modern edition of it exists which contains a detailed discussion of performance on appropriate instruments.[27]

Piano pedalling

Detailed information on the stops, knee levers and pedals of early pianos can be found in a number of sources.[28] A brief summary is given here.

The earliest pianos had stop mechanisms for varying their tone. Cristofori's pianos had a facility for sliding the keyboard laterally so that the hammer struck only one string per note – the *una corda*. Some other southern European pianos made in the Cristofori tradition also had the device.[29] Silbermann's pianos had a stop for raising the dampers from the strings (the precursor of the modern sustaining pedal) as well as a stop which brought small pieces of ivory into contact with the string, producing a harpsichord-like buzz.[30]

Towards the end of the eighteenth century a variety of stops, pedals and levers was available. On English grands, two pedals were customary; one for the *una corda* (which, on pianos with three strings per note, could be adjusted so that the hammer hit either one or two strings) and one for the damper-raising mechanism. It is less easy to generalise about grands on the continent, but many had knee levers after about 1780 for raising the dampers and some had a moderator stop or knee lever, which caused a strip of felt to be interposed between the hammer and strings.

Eighteenth-century square pianos were even less uniform in their disposition than grands. Some had no devices for altering the sound. Many, however, had a handstop, knee lever or pedal to operate the damper-raising mechanism, which was sometimes divided in the middle of the keyboard so that either treble or bass dampers could be raised independently of the others. Some also had a mechanism for making the sound quieter. On English squares, there was usually a harp or buff stop, which brought a strip of leather into permanent contact with the ends of the strings, producing a pizzicato effect. The buff was also found on continental squares, as was the moderator. Both in England and in continental Europe a swell mechanism that lifted part of the instrument's lid was sometimes incorporated in order to enhance the limited capabilities for dynamic contrasts: very occasionally it was used on grands too. Because of the design of squares, the *una corda* was difficult to fit, but a few English makers managed to do so.[31]

Early nineteenth-century English grand pianos, like their eighteenth-century counterparts, usually had pedals for just *una corda* and damper-raising. For the first two decades or so of the century the latter was divided, so that the treble and bass dampers could be raised separately, and occasionally makers included other pedals. However, English grands generally had fewer pedals than their continental counterparts in the period. 'Viennese' pianos in the period *c.* 1800–40 typically had four or five pedals – *una corda*, damper-raising, moderator (sometimes there were two moderators with differing degrees of muffling) and bassoon. The bassoon is found on some pianos at the end of the eighteenth century and it operates by bringing a strip of silk or parchment into contact with the bass strings, in order to produce a buzzing effect. In addition, a 'Turkish music' effect was sometimes possible through mechanisms that imitated drums, bells and cymbals. French grands also had four pedals in this period. These were often the same as the four found on Viennese grands, although the bassoon was sometimes omitted in favour of a buff, or harp pedal. Throughout the period, it is impossible to generalise about the disposition of squares.

The third ('sostenuto') pedal found on modern grands was patented in 1875 by Steinway, following three decades of experimentation with selective damper-raising devices. The third pedal was not wholeheartedly adopted by European makers.

Prior to the appearance of pedal markings in some printed music of the 1790s the sources of information on the subject are to be found in keyboard tutors and other documentary sources. These sources suggest that the earliest pianists thought of the various stops, levers and pedals at their disposal in much the same way as harpsichord registers had been regarded – they were generally to be used for whole movements, or sections of works. This might in any case have been surmised, since so many early instruments are

Ex. 4.2 Mozart, Sonata in D, K.311 (284c), second movement, bars 86–90

equipped with handstops that could only be operated in convenient breaks in the music, when the hands were free to leave the keyboard. Even the damper-raising device was used like this: eighteenth-century ears must have been able to tolerate a significant amount of harmonic blurring. C. P. E. Bach wrote:

> The undamped register of the fortepiano is the most pleasing and, once the performer learns to observe the necessary precautions in the face of its reverberations, the most delightful for improvisation.[32]

Charles Burney heard Madame Brillon play in Paris in 1770:

> After coffee we went into the music room where I found an English pianoforte which Mr Bach had sent her . . . I could not persuade Madame B. to play the piano forte with the stops on – *c'est sec*, she said – but with them off unless in arpeggios, nothing is distinct – 'tis like the sound of bells, continual and confluent.[33]

Whether the damper-raising pedal or knee lever was used in the eighteenth century for shorter passages of a few beats is unclear. The absence of any references to this practice in the contemporary literature, as well as the nature of the earliest pedal markings (see below), suggests that any such use would have been unusual. However, a few rare examples of keyboard notation suggest that the sustaining lever or pedal may have been depressed for short periods at an early date (Ex. 4.2).

The effects of performing with various stops, levers or pedals engaged were often compared in the eighteenth century with effects produced by other instruments. The use of the damper-raising device to imitate the pantalon (see p. 35 above) was common, but other effects are also described in

Ex. 4.3 Boieldieu, *1er Concerto*, last movement, 3rd variation, bars 1–2

the literature. The list in Milchmeyer's tutor of 1797 is probably the most comprehensive and includes effects such as bells, vocal duets, Spanish music, the harmonica, tambourine and mandolin.[34] However, many musicians were sceptical of the value of these effects and preferred to use none of them.[35] If later sources are to be believed (and notwithstanding passages such as Ex. 4.2), it is unlikely that Mozart, for example, used stops or levers very much.

A very small number of indications for some of the piano's registers occur prior to the 1790s, but from 1793 onwards music with pedalling indications was published regularly, first in Paris, then in London (from 1797) and shortly afterwards in Vienna. The first works to be published with comprehensive pedalling were the *6me Pot Pourri . . .* and the *Mélange*, Op. 10 of Daniel Steibelt, both written with square pianos in mind and both published in Paris in 1793. In these works lengthy sections of music are to be played with the pedals depressed throughout. It might be argued that these markings are not to be taken literally, and that they merely outline the sections during which a pedal is depressed and raised several times. In the case of the damper-raising pedal, this would prevent any blurring of the harmonies. However, other markings of the period demonstrate that composers of the time really did envisage whole sections being played without the release of the damper-raising pedal. The twelve-bar third variation from the last movement of Boieldieu's *1er Concerto* is an example, at the beginning of which is the instruction 'damper-raising pedal for the whole variation. "Sourdine" for the chords only' ('Grande Pedalle toute la Variation. Sourdine aux accords seulement' – Ex. 4.3). In the light of markings such as these, a literal interpretation on an early Viennese piano of Beethoven's direction to play the whole of the first movement of the Sonata, Op. 27, No. 2 (the 'Moonlight') with the dampers raised throughout appears to be stylistically

Ex. 4.4 Beethoven, Sonata in A♭, Marcia funebre, bar 31

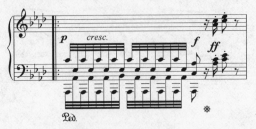

appropriate. (Performance of this movement with the dampers raised throughout on a later piano is not really appropriate because of the increased resonance and lack of clarity in the bass.)

Among early pedal markings, those for the damper-raising device predominate. They are often identified with recurring themes (for example, in the last movement of Beethoven's 'Waldstein' Sonata, Op. 53, where the sustaining device lends a particular character to the rondo theme), with passages of arpeggios and broken chords and with rapidly-repeated notes (Ex. 4.4). In music from the end of the 1790s the damper-raising pedal is often used for a new kind of piano texture in which the accompaniment is spread out well beyond the reach of the left hand (Ex. 4.5). This effect is very significant as it marks a point at which composers began to write textures for the piano that are unrealisable on the harpsichord or clavichord. Very occasionally, among early pedal markings, the damper-raising pedal's specific purpose seems to be to add 'warmth' to a short passage in a way that is familiar to modern performers; but this is rare.

Early nineteenth-century tutors comment on the differing degrees to which certain schools of pianists used the pedals. The 'London' school, especially Dussek, were regarded as pioneers, but the 'Viennese', such as Hummel, were regarded as very conservative. This pattern is found in the music itself, and those individuals who performed in London and Paris, in particular, often relied more heavily on the pedals than pianists elsewhere. There were exceptions: Beethoven, for example, seems to have played more in the style of the 'London school'.

As the sustaining pedal came to be used with greater frequency, so the technique of its use became more sophisticated. Dussek's use of it in Paris around the end of the first decade of the nineteenth century was especially noteworthy:

Ex. 4.5 Dussek, Sonata in B♭, Op. 39, No. 3, second movement, bars 82–3

Now, how Dussek used it; that was at first a mystery; and while some said that he never left it, others claimed, with some reason, that he made it move like the handle of a knife-grinder.[36]

This suggests that Dussek used syncopated pedalling (in which the pedal is released just as the harmony changes – usually on the beat – and is immediately depressed again). The effect must have been to produce a kind of 'super legato' that was not possible with the fingers alone. Some of Clementi's very carefully marked scores from the second decade of the nineteenth century also indicate the use of syncopated pedalling (Fig. 4.1).

The use of pedals other than that which raised the dampers was controversial at the beginning of the nineteenth century. Beethoven, in particular, used the *una corda* extensively, but others preferred to ignore it, because it was perceived as changing the tone of the piano and sending it out of tune. Very few markings exist for the moderator, although it features in a number of works by Schubert (see the 'con sordini' indications in the A minor Sonata, D.748). Other pedals, especially those that operated the 'Turkish' effects, were strongly denounced in the didactic literature.

In the second quarter of the nineteenth century Paris, the home of so many prominent virtuosos (including Chopin and Liszt), was perceived as encouraging a very extravagant style of playing characterised by wild gestures, rhythmic waywardness and copious pedalling. Liszt epitomised this spirit, whereas Chopin was renowned for the subtlety of his pedalling. In contrast, some German pianists were much more conservative in their playing styles. One of the most notable of these was Wieck, teacher of both Robert and Clara Schumann, and father of the latter.

Pedal markings in scores of the nineteenth century do not necessarily give a true picture of the extent to which a work should be pedalled. There are several reasons why pedalling was only approximately notated, or omitted altogether,

Fig. 4.1 Clementi's *Fantasia*, Op. 48, bars 16–22. The systematic positioning of the pedal release sign beneath the first and third beats of the bar strongly suggest syncopated pedalling.

ranging from composers' laziness to the difficulties of notating pedalling with adequate precision. Commentators on the performances of most of the major figures in the early nineteenth century remarked that they used the pedals in a far more sophisticated and extensive way than is indicated in their music.

Hand position and finger technique

From the late sixteenth to the early nineteenth centuries there was a high degree of uniformity in the hand positions and other aspects of technique adopted by performers.[37] Many writers during this period make remarks similar to those of C. P. E. Bach, stressing the need for a technique in which there is very little movement of anything but the fingers:

10. The performer must sit at the middle of the keyboard so that he may strike the highest as well as the lowest notes with equal ease.
11. When the performer is in the correct position with respect to height his forearms are suspended slightly above the fingerboard.
12. In playing, the fingers should be arched and the muscles relaxed . . . This can be observed immediately in a performer: if he understands the correct principles of fingering and has not acquired the habit of making unnecessary gestures, he will play the most difficult things in such a manner that the motion of his hands will be barely noticeable . . .[38]

The principles of a good technique that are articulated in C. P. E. Bach's treatise were taught him by his father, whose remarkable playing style is described in a number of sources, including Forkel:

> Sebastian Bach is said to have played with so easy and small a motion of the fingers that it was hardly perceptible. Only the first joints of the fingers were in motion; the hand retained even in the most difficult passages its rounded form; the fingers rose very little from the keys, hardly more than in a shake [trill], and when one was employed, the other remained quietly in its position. Still less did the other parts of his body take any share in his play, as happens with many whose hand is not light enough.[39]

Burney's description of Handel's technique is similar: 'his touch was so smooth and the tone of the instrument so cherished that his fingers seemed to grow to the keys. They were so curved and compact that when he played no motion and scarcely the fingers themselves could be discovered.'[40]

There are small variations in eighteenth-century descriptions of technique that probably relate to the fact that different national and regional traditions of playing were based on the experience of playing different instruments. In Germany, the clavichord was considered to be the best instrument on which to learn. Sources that originated there tend to describe the keys as 'stroked', or 'pressed', rather than struck – an obvious necessity, since any noise that results from the fingers hitting the keys causes a distraction on such a quiet instrument. According to Forkel, Bach's technique was based on this approach:

> no finger must fall upon its key, or . . . be thrown upon it, but only needs to be *placed* upon it . . . The impulse thus given to the keys, or the quantity of pressure, must be maintained in equal strength, and that in such a manner that the finger be not raised perpendicularly from the key, but that it glide off the forepart of the key, by gradually drawing back the tip of the finger towards the palm of the hand.[41]

Elsewhere, authors such as Rameau, who seem to have in mind the resistance that is created as the harpsichord plectrum comes into contact with the string, describe the fingers as 'dropping' onto the keys (but not 'hitting' them).[42]

Since neither the key resistance nor the key depth of early pianos is appreciably greater than that of earlier keyboard instruments it is not surprising that quiet hand positions and techniques based on minimal curved finger movement continued to be used in the late eighteenth and early nineteenth centuries. Mozart's often-quoted criticism of Nannette Stein indicates his preference for a quiet finger technique:

> instead of sitting in the middle of the clavier, she sits right up opposite the treble, as it gives her more chance of flopping about and making grimaces . . . When a passage is being played, the arm must be raised as high as possible, and according as the notes in the passage are stressed, the arm, not the fingers, must do this, and that too with great emphasis in a heavy and clumsy manner.[43]

Beethoven's technique, despite the vigour of much of his writing for the keyboard, was evidently based on a similar approach: 'Beethoven played with his hands so very still; wonderful as his execution was, there was no tossing of them to and fro, up and down; they seemed to glide right and left over the keys, the fingers alone doing the work.'[44] The keyboard tutors of Milchmeyer (1797), Adam (1804), Hummel (1828) and many others advocate a similarly quiet hand position and finger technique. However, as piano actions became heavier and the depth of touch became greater a different approach was required. These features of the instrument itself, along with a musical style increasingly based on thicker textures, octave passages, etc., meant that the wrist and arm were increasingly brought into play.

Fingering and keyboard touch

There are many examples of fingerings in early sources, chiefly in scores that were used for teaching purposes. These sources tell us much about early keyboard techniques, and at the same time reveal a great deal about the appropriate articulation of early keyboard music. Modern performers who wish to use early fingerings will find a useful starting point in the anthology assembled by Lindley and Boxall.[45] Early fingerings also exist in editions of music by individual composers and they are discussed in the literature on early keyboard performance. A summary of some of the most useful sources is given here.[46]

There are many examples of early fingerings in the music of the English virginalists.[47] Continental fingerings from a similar period are found in Sweelinck's music (see in particular the Fantasia and toccatas L14, 15, 18, 19, 21 and 22), although it is uncertain whether the fingering originated with the composer.[48] A number of eighteenth-century sources of fingering have been studied in detail. The extensive fingerings of Alessandro Scarlatti have been used to cast light on his son Domenico's performing style.[49] Three sources of J. S. Bach's music are fingered: the *Applicatio* (BWV 994) and *Praeambulum* (BWV 930) from Wilhelm Friedemann's notebook and an early version of the first prelude and fugue from Book 2 of the '48' (BWV 870a – written down by Bach's pupil Johann Caspar Vogler). There is very little original fingering in the music of Haydn and Mozart (two sonatas by Haydn and a few finger studies by Mozart[50]), but there are many more in sources associated with Beethoven and Clementi which are discussed by Rosenblum and others.[51] Among the more noteworthy nineteenth-century fingerings are those of Field and Chopin.[52]

Fundamental to the performance practices of sixteenth- and seventeenth-century keyboard players were the use of paired fingerings and the relatively sparing use of the thumb and fifth finger. The use of the same finger on successive notes separated by an interval was also common, but finger-substitution was very rare. All of these features continued into the eighteenth century, which was, however, a period of transition, by the end of which the essentials of modern fingering had been established.

Typical of the kind of paired scale fingerings that were used in the sixteenth and seventeenth centuries were, for the right hand 343434 (ascending) and 323232 (descending) and for the left hand 43214321 (ascending) and 12343434 (descending). A number of general observations can be made about these fingerings. First, there is a common identification in the sources of 'strong' fingers with 'strong' notes. In the particular right-hand fingering patterns referred to above, 3 is identified as 'strong', while both 2 and 4 are 'weak', assuming that scale patterns are of notes grouped in twos or fours (which is the usual way in which scales are presented in the sources). The identification of 3 as strong was common, but not universal; some sources make 3 'weak', and 2 and 4 'strong'. Secondly, the use of the thumb in early scale fingerings is limited: it is found only in the left-hand scale fingering (in some sources it is paired with 2 in scale passages). This feature of early scale

Ex. 4.6 Bull, Fantasia in D minor, bars 1–3 (right-hand part)

fingerings relates to what we know of early hand positions, in which the thumb was not necessarily held in readiness above the keys as it is in a modern technique, but held a little back from the keys, towards the performer. (The shortness of the keys of early keyboards means that it is in any case more difficult for the thumb to be placed above the keys if a relaxed hand position is maintained.) Thirdly, 5 is absent from these scale fingerings – an almost universal feature. Finally, in order to achieve paired fingerings such as those described above it is clear that the wrist cannot stay in the same position for upward- and downward-moving scales. Depending on the fingering pattern, the hand must be oriented either away from the performer, or towards the centre of the keyboard. In an ascending passage using 3434 . . ., for example, the right hand needs to swivel to the right so that the fingers can 'walk' easily towards the top of the keyboard. Similarly, for a 3232 descending right-hand scale, the right hand will need to be made to point towards the centre of the keyboard to allow a similar type of motion. Orientation of the hands in these ways permits a relatively smooth performance, rather than the exaggerated articulation in pairs that is assumed by some to be the consequence of paired fingerings.

While certain principles of early fingering can be deduced from the didactic literature, fingered pieces of music demonstrate how those principles work out in practice. They also raise matters that are seldom addressed in the treatises. Example 4.6 (for the right hand), the source of which dates from the 1630s, illustrates a number of points. It is clear in this example that 3 was considered to be strong – it is used on almost all of the important beats, or subdivisions of beats. The use of the same finger on successive notes separated by a wide interval, as in bar 1 of Example 4.6, is common in sources up to the eighteenth century and indicates an articulated style. The example also shows that the fifth finger was used, particularly in the context of leaps, even though it is not generally found in scale fingerings.

Bars 19 and 20 of a Gibbons Fantasia demonstrate a few additional features of early fingering (Ex. 4. 7). The paired left-hand fingerings in bar 20 are typical, as is the repeated use of the thumb in the 'alto' part, where a

Ex. 4.7 Gibbons, Fantasia in A minor, bars 19–20

Ex. 4.8 J. S. Bach, *Applicatio*, BWV 994, bars 1–2

Ex. 4.9 J. S. Bach, Prelude in C, BWV 870a, bar 4

modern performer would probably attempt a more legato style by using 2 alongside 1, or finger-substitution.

The paired fingerings of earlier centuries were still in use in J. S. Bach's time, as his *Applicatio* for Wilhelm Friedemann shows (Ex. 4.8). The articulated style created by the use of the same finger on successive notes (particularly in inner parts) is also found in fingered sources associated with Bach. Example 4.9 shows how the inner parts are largely played with the thumbs of both hands, enabling a more relaxed hand position to be maintained than if finger substitution was used to play these parts *legato*. Yet at the same time as he was teaching and using traditional methods, J. S. Bach was developing a new style of fingering in which, among other things, the thumb was assuming a more prominent role than previously.[53]

C. P. E. Bach's treatise contains evidence of fingering patterns in transition: many of his illustrations are given with alternative fingerings (Ex. 4.10). Here, scale patterns in which the thumb is taken after chromatic notes and in the middle of natural-key passages in the modern thumbs-under

Ex. 4.10 C. P. E. Bach, *Versuch*, vol. I, Chapter 1, Figure 8. The asterisked fingerings are described by Bach as the least usual.

Ex. 4.11 F. Couperin, *L'Art de toucher le clavecin*

Ex. 4.12 F. Couperin, *L'Art de toucher le clavecin*

Ex. 4.13 F. Couperin, *L'Art de toucher le clavecin*, Premier Prélude, bars 1–4

manner emerge alongside fingerings that are still dependent on the old paired principles. By this time the old paired fingerings were considered to be outmoded by many and they became increasingly rare as the century wore on, and as modern fingering patterns began to become established.

A number of other changes took place in the eighteenth century that were designed to create a smoother keyboard style. In François Couperin's *L'Art de toucher le clavecin* (Paris, 1717), for example, the 'old style' of playing consecutive thirds with the same fingers (Ex. 4.11) is replaced by the 'modern' way of performing them with different fingers (Ex. 4.12). The fingered preludes that form part of Couperin's treatise also demonstrate a technique in which finger-substitution features more prominently than it had among Couperin's predecessors and many of his contemporaries (Ex. 4.13). (Despite the articulated style of Example 4.9, one or two examples of finger substitution are also found in J. S. Bach's C major prelude and fugue from Book 2 of the '48', BWV 870a.)

Modern principles of fingering are clearly described in keyboard tutors of the late eighteenth century. Among these was Türk's influential *Klavierschule*, in which he enumerates several rules for good fingering:

> One is only rarely permitted to put the little fingers and the thumbs of both hands on a raised key, unless the passage in question is such that no other way of playing it is possible . . .
>
> One may not strike two successive keys with one finger . . .
>
> When the fingers of the right hand are not sufficient for an ascending passage, then one places the thumb in a manner appropriate to the context, either under the second, third, or fourth finger . . . This very ordinary device, by means of which the keyboard player can gain a number of fingers sufficient for playing passages extending several octaves, is called 'putting the thumb under' . . .
>
> If the fingers of the right hand are not sufficient for descending passages, then the second, third, or fourth finger goes over the thumb . . .
>
> The thumb may be effectively used immediately before or after a raised key
>
> The fingers are used in succession, without leaving one out, when the given passage is in stepwise motion . . .
>
> When a tone is sustained for a longer amount of time, it is sometimes necessary to change fingers while holding a key down . . .[54]

Similar principles apply to left-hand passages and Türk also elaborates on the performance of skips. Passages based on this kind of fingering will be found in other tutors of the period and in the music of Clementi, Beethoven and their contemporaries. Occasionally, for a particular expressive effect, a composer such as Beethoven or Chopin indicates fingering that is contrary to one of the accepted rules. The use of the same finger on successive melody notes in a delicate right-hand passage, for example, is quite a common occurrence. However, these exceptions to the rules should not divert attention from the fact that all of the major pianists of the late eighteenth and early nineteenth centuries set great store by the general adherence to principles that had by then become established.

The changes in fingering that took place in the eighteenth century are related to a more general trend that included string and woodwind playing[55] which saw a movement away from a clearly-articulated style towards performances that were chiefly characterised by legato playing. Marpurg's comments are typical of the general approach in the mid-eighteenth century:

> In contrast to the legato and staccato there is the ordinary manner of playing in which the finger is lifted from the key just before the following note is played. The ordinary manner of playing, since it is always taken for granted, is never marked.[56]

Sources of the period also make it clear that the extent of separation in performance depended on the speed and character of a movement – detached playing was considered to be better suited to faster rather than slower movements. Legato playing in the middle of the century was indicated by slurs or by the use of an Italian term.[57] A shift towards a greater emphasis on legato playing is evident in the increasing numbers of slurs found in keyboard scores during the second half of the eighteenth century. By the beginning of the nineteenth century a legato style was becoming more usual. In 1801 Clementi wrote:

> N.B. When the composer leaves the legato, and staccato to the performer's taste; the best rule is, to adhere chiefly to the legato; reserving the staccato to give spirit occasionally to certain passages, and to set off the higher beauties of the legato.[58]

That the change in style from Marpurg's 'ordinary manner' to Clementi's legato style was more than a very small shift in emphasis is suggested by comments such as those of Beethoven to his pupil Czerny:

> [Beethoven] went through the various keyboard studies in Bach's book and especially insisted on legato technique, which was one of the unforgettable features of his playing; at that time [just after 1800] all other pianists considered that kind of legato unattainable, since the *hammered*, detached staccato technique of Mozart's time was still *fashionable*. (Some years later Beethoven told me that he had heard Mozart play on several occasions and that, since at

that time the forte-piano was still in its infancy, Mozart, more accustomed to the then still prevalent *Flügel*, used a technique entirely unsuited for the fortepiano. . .).[59]

Some clavichord techniques

Bebung is an eighteenth-century German term used for a vibrato on the clavichord that is obtained by a variation of pressure on the key while the tangent is in contact with the strings. Evidence for the technique exists in the sixteenth and seventeenth centuries,[60] but it is in the eighteenth-century treatises (especially of Marpurg, C. P. E. Bach and Türk) that it receives its fullest descriptions.

The sources are agreed that *Bebung* can only be achieved properly on a good clavichord. In his section on ornaments Türk sums up most of the *Bebung*'s features:

> The *Bebung* . . . can only be used effectively over long notes, partic- ularly in compositions of melancholy character and the like. It is indicated by the sign at 'a' or by the word tremolo (b). The execu- tion must be approximately as in 'c' or 'd' . . . The finger is allowed to remain on the key for as long as is required by the duration of the given note and attempts to reinforce the tone with a repeated and gentle pressure . . . In general, one ought to beware of the fre- quent use of the *Bebung* and when it is used, one must guard against ugly exaggeration of the tone by too violent a pressure.[61]

Ex. 4.14 Türk, *Klavierschule* (1789), p. 293

The *Tragen der Töne* is an effect that is related to the *Bebung* in that it refers to those places where a particular pressure is exerted on the keys. C. P. E. Bach describes it in the following terms:

> The notes found in Fig. IV will be drawn out, and each of them receives in the same time a perceptible pressure. The slurring of

notes by a slur with dots is in fact known in keyboard terminology as *Tragen der Töne*.[62]

Ex. 4.15 C. P. E. Bach, *Versuch*, vol. I, Chapter 3, Figure IV

The effect appears 'to consist of a single variation of the pressure of the finger on a series of notes after each attack'.[63]

5   Non-notated and notated issues

Improvisation and preluding

Modern performers tend to play almost exclusively what has been notated by someone else, whereas musicians of the seventeenth, eighteenth and nineteenth centuries would have thought it odd not to be expected to improvise occasional movements, preludes or embellishments to melodies. Improvisation in one form or another is perhaps the most neglected aspect of early performance practices, and one that it is possible to revive by a study of the relevant sources.

There are numerous accounts from the seventeenth to the nineteenth centuries of keyboard players improvising complete works. For certain organists' posts in Germany the auditioning process required that performers should improvise preludes, fugues, chorale preludes or variations and chaconnes.[1] Bach used similar skills in a performance on one of Silbermann's pianos before Frederick the Great in 1747 when he improvised a fugue on a theme given to him by the King – an event that prompted the subsequent composition of the *Musical Offering*.[2] J. S. Bach's son Carl Philipp Emanuel was renowned for his improvisations[3] and included a substantial chapter on the subject in his treatise.[4] His advice largely has to do with the harmonic structure and figuration appropriate to free fantasias, although his comments are also relevant to the performance of preludes (see below). Mozart's skills are summed up in the account of a soirée at which he improvised on a theme 'for an hour in such a way as to excite general admiration and shew by means of variations and fugues . . . that he was master of every aspect of the musician's art'.[5] Beethoven was capable of comparable improvisations while other virtuosi of his generation embarrassed themselves publicly when attempting similar feats.[6]

Most modern keyboard players are unlikely to attempt such full-scale performances, but they might wish to develop their improvisation and figured-bass skills by playing continuo solos, or *partimenti*.[7] These consist only of a

Ex. 5.1 C. P. E. Bach, *Versuch*, Chapter 7

figured bass line above which free or contrapuntal textures are improvised. The process is similar to that of accompanying the solo line of an eighteenth-century sonata, except that the melody instrument is missing. Examples of continuo solos and *partimenti* exist by a number of composers including Durante, Leo, Cotumacci and Fenaroli, but the most accessible are the multi-movement sonatas by Bernardo Pasquini, which are available in a modern edition.[8]

Throughout almost the entire history of keyboard music the art of preluding has been an important element of improvised performance. An improvised prelude is a short, introductory passage or piece that is played immediately before a more substantial movement, or multi-movement work, setting the scene for the work that follows in both mood and key. Irrespective of their period, preludes tended to be rhythmically free and depended substantially on arpeggio, broken-chord and scale figurations. The tradition of preluding largely died out in the course of the twentieth century, but sufficient models exist for it to be revived in an historically appropriate way.

Many preludes exist among Handel's keyboard works and in suites by French Baroque composers and their imitators. François Couperin's *L'Art de toucher le clavecin* contains eight model preludes of varying degrees of difficulty. The composer notes that 'although these preludes are written in measured time, there is, nevertheless, a style, dictated by custom, which must be observed . . . A prelude is a free composition, in which the imagination gives rein to any fancy that may present itself . . . those who have recourse to these non-improvised preludes should play them in a free, easy style, not sticking too closely to the exact time, unless I have expressly indicated this by the word Mesuré.'[9]

C. P. E. Bach's chapter on improvisation is mostly devoted to the demands of larger-scale free fantasias, but his remarks suggest that many of the principles outlined in his chapter also apply to preluding. The style that he advocates is unmeasured and the framework for each improvisation is a figured-bass line (Ex. 5.1). Preludes, he says, should 'prepare the content of

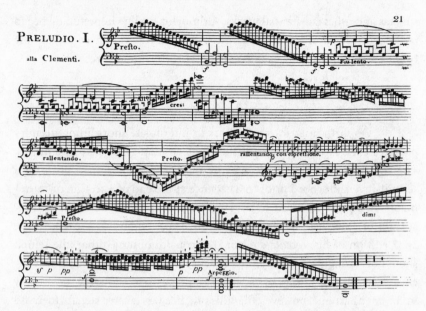

Fig. 5.1 'Preludio I, alla Clementi', from Clementi's *Musical characteristics*, p. 21

the piece that follows . . . the content or affect of this piece becomes the material out of which the prelude is fashioned'.[10]

Several references to the art of preluding survive from the late eighteenth and early nineteenth centuries. Five preludes by Mozart survive; the *Modulierendes Präludium (F–e)*, K.deest and four preludes that make up the work previously known as the Fantasia or Capriccio in C major, K.395 (bars 1–13, 14–19, 20–25 and 26 to the end). Four of Mozart's preludes start and end in different keys and between them they demonstrate a wide range of preluding practice. Some are quick and showy while others are more expressive, and they range in length from two systems to two or three pages of a modern score.

Clementi's *Musical characteristics* of 1787 were among the earliest of many late eighteenth- and nineteenth-century publications to include examples of preludes in different keys (Fig. 5.1). They are available in a modern edition.[11] Individuals such as Cramer, Hummel, Moscheles, Chaulieu, Czerny, Kalkbrenner and a host of others also provided examples that might be used appropriately to provide introductions to the modern performance of sonatas and other substantial works. Although a decline in preluding began in the second half of the nineteenth century, the tradition lived on into the twentieth. As late as 1938, examples by Josef Hofmann were recorded.[12]

Cadenzas, fermatas and lead-ins

Opportunities for performers to interpolate short, improvisatory passages exist in many works of the eighteenth and nineteenth centuries. The signal to do so is usually a pause mark, more often than not over a second-inversion chord prior to a cadence at the end of a section or movement. This practice seems to have grown out of the seventeenth-century custom of embellishing cadences, at which the tempo was slowed. In the 1637 edition of his *Toccate e partite* Frescobaldi observed that 'the tempo should be strongly retarded on the cadences . . . and equally, when the conclusion is near, the passage or cadence should be played slower'.[13] It was only in the later Baroque, however, that this practice was taken a step further and pause marks were used to indicate improvised cadenzas.

Many opportunities exist for cadenzas in late Baroque vocal, string and wind music, especially in works of the Italian style. Cadenzas typically occur just before the final cadence of the soloist's part in either the A or B section of a *da capo* aria form or before the final *tutti* section of an instrumental concerto movement. In some slow movements there is a need for a brief improvisation before or on the final chord. Several specimen vocal and instrumental cadenzas exist from the first half of the eighteenth century, and the subject is discussed in some detail in contemporary treatises as well as in the modern literature.[14]

Keyboard music of the same period offers fewer opportunities for improvisation, largely because the repertory of the first half of the eighteenth century tended to be written in forms and styles other than those mentioned in the previous paragraph. Nevertheless, short cadenzas are sometimes appropriate. Works written in the Italian sonata style for solo keyboard, or for melody instrument with keyboard obbligato, occasionally require brief cadenzas at unembellished pauses, or chords followed by rests, at structurally significant moments. Examples can be found in works such as Telemann's fantasias (which, despite their titles, are stylistically similar to numerous sonatas of the Baroque). Frederick Neumann, while acknowledging that there are few places in Bach's music where passages may be interpolated, has pointed out a few 'gaps' that may need to be filled, such as the last two chords of the first movement of the Sonata in G for viola da gamba and harpsichord, BWV 1027.[15] A striking example of a realised, but improvisatory passage interpolated at the final (imperfect) cadence of a slow movement occurs in the Adagio (third movement) of Handel's F major Suite, HWV 427.

Despite the popularity of the concerto in the late Baroque, very few were written for harpsichord.[16] Bach was a pioneer in the genre, but there is very little scope for improvisation in most of his keyboard concertos. The cadenza to the first movement of the fifth Brandenburg Concerto is much lengthier than other instrumental or vocal models of the period and leaves no room for additions. There are also brief, written-out cadenzas at the pauses in bars 272–3 of the last movement of the D minor Concerto, BWV 1052 and at bars 121–2 of the first movement of the D major Concerto, BWV 1054. However, opportunities for brief, improvised cadenzas exist at the pauses in bar 22 of the second movement of the D major Concerto, BWV 1054 and at bar 196 of the last movement of the F minor Concerto, BWV 1056.

A number of fugal movements of the early eighteenth century have pauses just before the final cadence. In the penultimate bar of the two-part 'Canon alla Decima' from Bach's *Art of Fugue* the direction 'Cadenza' is found alongside a pause over a second-inversion chord. Some of Handel's keyboard fugues also have pauses, or rests following chords just before the end, at which it seems likely that short cadenzas were intended.

Keyboard music of the mid-eighteenth century offers more frequent opportunities for improvisation than the earlier repertory. C. P. E. Bach, in the first part of his keyboard tutor (1753), discusses the elaboration of fermatas which, he says, usually occur in slow movements and which 'must be embellished if only to avoid artlessness'.[17] He includes a number of specimen examples of elaborations, all of them brief: half of one of the most extensive is included here as Example 5.2. (Example 5.2a is realised as Example 5.2b.) The earlier sonatas of Haydn, as well as those of his contemporaries such as J. C. Bach, contain several instances where a pause mark indicates a brief elaboration.[18] Later Classical works, however, including Haydn's later sonatas, tend to be more comprehensively notated, so that there is less scope for brief cadenzas. Türk's remarks in 1789, which are more

Ex. 5.2 C. P. E. Bach, *Versuch*, Chapter 2

guarded than those of C. P. E. Bach, are in line with the trend towards more prescriptive notation: he commented that fermatas could be played either with or without embellishment, and that an embellished fermata was an appropriate thing 'now and then'.[19]

Almost without exception, each of the numerous keyboard concertos of the Classical era contains one or more opportunities for a cadenza. For concertos by well-known composers there is often (but not always) one or more surviving sets of cadenzas, but for works by lesser composers, especially of the eighteenth century, there are often none. Where no original cadenza survives a later composer or editor may have supplied one, but in many cases the new cadenzas are stylistically inappropriate to the work for which they were composed. A number of nineteenth-century cadenzas (including some by Beethoven) were written for Mozart's concertos, for example, which are much lengthier than their eighteenth-century counterparts and in a harmonic and pianistic style that bears little resemblance to the works to which they were attached.

From existing cadenzas and from keyboard tutors it is possible to arrive at some stylistic guidelines for the improvisation or composition of Classical cadenzas. There are three original cadenzas for each of the first two movements of Mozart's Concerto in C, K.246, for example, dating from the period *c.* 1777–82.[20] The earliest cadenzas are short – each occupying no more than two systems of a modern score – and comprise figuration (mostly for the right hand) that bears little or no relationship to the thematic content of their respective movements. The next cadenzas to be composed for the same two movements are approximately twice as long as the earliest examples. The latest of Mozart's cadenzas for the work are twice as long again and contain thematic material from the movements to which they are attached. Their style is entirely in accordance with Türk's advice on cadenzas published at about the same time. In outline, Türk's advice for an appropriate cadenza is:

- it should contain a brief summary of the most important elements of the movement, without undue repetition
- it should be in character with the movement, and not unnecessarily difficult
- it should not be too long (the advice to singers and woodwind players earlier in the century had been that a cadenza should only require one breath)
- any modulation should be brief, and not to a remote key (especially if that key has not been used in the movement)
- it should contain elements of surprise, novelty, wit and an abundance of ideas
- dissonances should be resolved properly
- the tempo should be flexible
- it should sound as if it has been improvised.[21]

Embellishment

In a frequently-quoted passage of 1752 Quantz wrote, 'The *Italian manner of playing* . . . permits many additions of graces, and requires a seemly knowledge of harmony . . . The *French manner of playing* . . . does not require much knowledge of harmony, since the embellishments are generally prescribed by the composer.'[22] This is an extremely broad generalisation that can nevertheless be applied to much of the repertory. Keyboard music in the Italian style does indeed often require embellishment while French Baroque music usually contains the composer's copious directions for ornamentation. François Couperin, for example, insisted that nothing should be added: 'I declare that my pieces must be performed just as I have written them and that they will never make much of an impression on people of genuine taste unless all my markings are observed to the letter.'[23] There are, however, several exceptions to Quantz's general rule. Early French harpsichord music, especially when the sources are manuscripts rather than printed editions, leaves plenty of room for additions (see Chapter 6), whereas some well-known examples of keyboard music in the Italian style, such as the slow movement of Bach's *Italian Concerto*, BWV 971 includes very carefully worked elaborations.

Of all the different types of movement in the Baroque, it was most usual for slow, Italianate arias to be most heavily embellished. Many vocal and instrumental models exist, as well as some particularly elaborate movements in Handel's suites – the first-movement Adagio of the F major Suite, HWV 427 and the Air of the D minor Suite, HWV 428 (for which there are two highly decorated versions of the earlier, plain Aria of the Suite, HWV 449). These examples provide models for the way in which similar, unornamented movements may be embellished.

In addition to the extensive style of embellishment required in some Italianate slow movements, there are many places in Baroque keyboard works where it is appropriate to add individual ornaments – trills, appoggiaturas, etc. Evidence for this practice is found in those numerous instances of works for which more than one early source exists. Frequently, two or more sources of the same work are ornamented differently, though not necessarily to the same extent, suggesting that composers were far from rigid in their views about a work's ornamentation. For any individual work, the extent to which a performer should add ornaments will depend on the style of a passage – melodic writing is more likely to be embellished than more complex textures – and the degree of precision with which the score has been notated.

Despite its frequent abuse,[24] the Baroque practice of embellishment was carried forward into the middle of the eighteenth century. As previously, slow movements of sonatas were particularly suited to embellishment, but sections of faster movements were also varied when they were repeated. In 1789 Türk (who also included in his tutor some specimen embellishments) summed up the circumstances in which keyboard players might elaborate a musical text:

> It may generally be observed . . . that only those places should be varied (but only when the composition is repeated) which would otherwise not be interesting enough and consequently become tedious . . . in general it is customary now and then to vary a passage at the repetition of an Allegro, and the like. However, longer elaborations are most frequently used in compositions of a gentle, pleasing character in slow tempo, and particularly in an Adagio.[25]

C. P. E. Bach's *Sonaten für Clavier mit veränderten Reprisen* (keyboard sonatas with varied reprises) of 1760 (Wq 50) demonstrate how the composer wanted his works to be embellished. They contain elaborations for repeated sections in both fast and slow movements. A copy, annotated by the composer, contains further embellishments and is reproduced in Garland's facsimile edition of the work.[26] The embellishments of Mozart's slow movements provide further models (see Exx. 2.2 and 2.3). However, despite the fact that embellishment was a common practice of the mid-eighteenth century, not all movements require the same amount of elaboration. As the century wore on composers tended to write into the score the elaborations they required – a situation that is implicitly recognised in Türk's somewhat guarded comments quoted above ('it is customary *now and then*'). In Haydn's case, while there is ample scope for additions in the earliest sonatas, many of those written after *c.* 1766 contain written-out embellishments by the composer. Repeated motifs and phrases, recapitulated passages and repeated sections are all found in variant form in the later sonatas, providing models of the kind of elaboration that the composer might have expected in unembellished works.[27]

The extent to which it is appropriate to embellish Mozart's music and the mature works of Haydn has been debated. In *The Classical style* Charles Rosen proclaimed that 'the music of Haydn after 1775 cannot be ornamented'.[28] Many modern scholars and performers have echoed these views, which were expressed as early as 1797 by Johann Peter Milchmeyer:

> I would like to ask the amateurs of the pianoforte to abstain from all ornaments of musical passages not given by the composer . . . Neither professionals, nor amateurs, nor beginners should play anything but the music of great masters, and then should not add the slightest of their own to it.[29]

In many works of the period extensive embellishments are indeed supplied by the composer (see, for example, the returns of the theme in Mozart's Rondo in A minor, K.511). Nevertheless, there are places in the mature works of Mozart and Haydn where repeated themes remain unembellished, suggesting to a number of recent scholars and performers that they should be elaborated.[30] Levin, for example, notes that 'it would seem illogical upon stylistic and expressive grounds for the theme of the second movement to the Sonata in B♭, K570, to be performed six times in succession . . . in a single, unadorned state'.[31]

Beethoven and his successors generally wrote in the score what they expected performers of their music to play. When Beethoven's pupil Czerny elaborated the composer's Piano Quintet, Op.16 during a performance in 1816 Beethoven objected strongly. The following day Beethoven wrote 'I burst out with that remark yesterday and I was very sorry after I had done so. But you must forgive a composer who would rather have heard his work performed exactly as it is written.'[32] Later, in 1828, Hummel noted that 'in Sonatas or variations of the present day, the Composer generally supplies the player with the required embellishment'.[33] Nevertheless, some performers persisted in elaborating the composer's text and the practice of pianists such as Chopin, who decorated some of his own melodies (see Chapter 6), suggests that embellishment of nineteenth-century scores should occasionally be considered.

Tempo fluctuation and tempo rubato

A useful summary of the subject will be found in Hudson's *Stolen time*.[34]

In the early Baroque, with the advent of overtly expressive monodic and madrigal styles, tempo flexibility was seen as an expressive tool, the tempo varying according to the meaning of the text. Sources from all over Europe attest to the practice[35] and it was evidently considered to be appropriate in some instrumental music, especially in works that were improvisatory in character (see above for some of Frescobaldi's remarks on the performance of toccatas). François Couperin's comments on the performance of preludes refer to a 'free, easy style, not sticking too closely to the exact time'[36] and J. S. Bach used the term *con discrezione* in the Adagio of his Toccata in D major, BWV 912. The term *discrétion* is also used in Froberger's keyboard music at the expressive ending to the *Tombeau de Monsieur Blancrocher*, and towards the end of some of his gigues, suggesting that he allowed for tempo flexibility even in works that are not improvisatory in character. This aspect of Froberger's style may have reflected a more general French tendency towards tempo flexibility. In 1754 Rameau commented on the need for the expression of feeling through a flexible approach to tempo and in 1768 an article in Rousseau's *Dictionnaire* contrasted the vagueness of the French beat to the precision of the Italian.[37]

Ex. 5.3 C. P. E. Bach, *Versuch*, Chapter 3

The tradition of tempo flexibility in music of an improvisatory character
– fantasias, cadenzas, etc. – continued after the middle of the eighteenth
century.[38] A degree of flexibility was also practised in other sorts of music,
although almost all writers of the late eighteenth and early nineteenth centuries are careful to warn against its excessive use. Flexibility was of two
kinds: lingering over certain notes in order to stress their importance and a
more gradual slowing or accelerating of the tempo over a more extended
period of time. C. P. E. Bach remarked on both sorts:

> [Example 5.3] contains several examples in which certain notes
> and rests should be extended beyond their written length, for
> affective reasons . . . they are indicated by a small cross . . . In
> general the retard fits slow or moderate tempos better than very
> fast ones . . . In affettuoso playing, the performer must avoid fre-
> quent and excessive retards, which tend to make the tempo drag.
> Hence every effort must be made despite the beauty of detail to
> keep the tempo at the end of a piece exactly the same as at the
> beginning, an extremely difficult assignment . . . Passages in a piece
> in major mode which are repeated in the minor may be broadened
> somewhat on their repetition in order to heighten the effect. On
> entering a fermata expressive of languidness, tenderness, or
> sadness, it is customary to broaden slightly.[39]

Bach's remarks are paralleled in several other sources of the late eighteenth
century, a number of which are summarised in Rosenblum's survey.[40] In
addition to slowing the tempo, typically for particularly expressive melodies,
Türk and others allow for a quickening of the tempo in more agitated passages.[41] Rosenblum has shown, however, that a slowing down followed by *a
tempo* is by far the most usual pattern of tempo flexibility in the period.

Not all late eighteenth-century keyboard players treated the tempo
flexibly to an equal extent. The Mozart household was particularly sensitive
to the issue. Leopold Mozart stressed the need for a strictly rhythmical

performance in his violin treatise[42] and his son's comments on a performance by Nannette Stein are in a similar vein:

> When a passage is repeated, she plays it more slowly the second time. If it has to be played a third time, then she plays it even more slowly . . . she will never acquire the most essential, the most difficult and the chief requisite in music, which is, time.[43]

Mozart's caution is reflected by the relative lack of gradual tempo changes in his music compared with that of, for example, Haydn.

Mozart's pupil, Hummel, one of the most conservative of the early nineteenth-century pianists, took on many aspects of his teacher's playing and in his piano tutor of 1828 criticised the 'capricious dragging or slackening of the time . . . introduced at every instant and to satiety' by some of his contemporaries. Even so, he allowed for a 'little relaxation as to time' in 'singing passages', while insisting that 'we must not deviate too strikingly from the predominating movement' and that the tempo should 'not waver in the time in every bar'.[44] By comparison with Hummel's playing, Beethoven's was generally considered by his contemporaries to be less restrained. Although it is difficult to be certain as to the extent of his flexibility in the tempo, some idea can be gained from Ries's description: 'generally he himself played his compositions very impetuously, yet for the most part stayed strictly in time, only infrequently pushing the tempo a little. Occasionally he would retard during a crescendo, which created a very beautiful and most remarkable effect.'[45]

Despite the concern of many early nineteenth-century pianists not to vary the tempo to excess, some pianists went much further. The most extreme styles of piano playing in the first half of the century were associated with Paris and although some pianists who lived there (such as Chopin) adopted a fairly restrained style, others most certainly did not. Mendelssohn deplored 'the Parisian tendency of overdoing passion and despair'[46] and Robert Schumann's father-in-law, Friedrich Wieck, described the rhythmic waywardness of the imaginary Paris-based virtuoso, Herr Forte:

> He didn't learn at all. He is a genius. It all comes naturally. Instruction would have chained his genius, and he would then play distinctly, correctly, naturally, and in time. That would be dilettantish. This unrhythmical and indisciplined hubbub is what is called 'inspired pianistic genius'.[47]

Ex. 5.4 F. Couperin, *L'Art de toucher le clavecin*

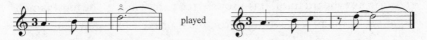

The most famous pianist of all to be associated with Paris was Franz Liszt, who is known to have had a very flexible approach to the tempo in his playing (see Fig. 2.2).[48]

Tempo rubato literally means 'robbed' or 'stolen time'. In *tempo rubato* the value of one note is taken away and given to another (or transferred to a rest). Typically, *tempo rubato* happens in melodic lines, so that in keyboard performance it leads to non-synchronisation between one hand (playing the melody) and the other (playing the accompaniment).

A number of Baroque sources refer to the practice of *tempo rubato* by singers and instrumentalists, but there are no specific references to it in the literature relating to keyboard performance before the middle of the eighteenth century. However, a parallel keyboard practice is described in French keyboard sources. François Couperin devised an ornament to be placed over an individual note (the 'suspension') whose effect was to delay the playing of that note (Ex. 5.4). He referred to it as an expressive effect and noted: 'as for the suspension, it is hardly employed at all except in slow and tender pieces. The duration of the rest which precedes the note over which it is marked must be left to the taste of the executant.'[49] The ornament does indeed occur only rarely in Couperin's music, but it was taken up by Rameau and seems to have been used with increasing frequency in French harpsichord music as the century progressed. In 1751 Foucquet wrote that 'in all pieces that require a gracious or tender execution, one ought to play the bass note before that of the melody, without altering the beat, which produces a suspension on each note of the melody'.[50] Couperin's and Rameau's ornaments, as well as Foucquet's comments, refer only to a performance style in which the left hand plays first: Forqueray in 1747 described both left-before-right as well as right-before-left performance.[51]

Despite the lack of references to *tempo rubato* in Baroque keyboard sources, the effect is sometimes built into the notation of movements such as the Andante of Bach's *Italian Concerto* (e.g. bar 40), suggesting that its use extended to keyboard players in Germany and elsewhere.

Marpurg in the 1750s was the first German theorist to describe *tempo rubato* in a keyboard tutor. It is also referred to by Türk.[52] The most famous exponent of the practice in the second half of the eighteenth century was Mozart, who remarked:

> Everyone is amazed that I can always keep strict time. What these people cannot grasp is that in tempo rubato in an Adagio, the left hand should go on playing in strict time. With them the left hand always follows suit.[53]

Some idea of Mozart's *rubato* style may be gained from an examination of those scores that were very carefully prepared by the composer – short extracts of rhythmically displaced melodic lines will be found in slow movements such as those of the sonatas K.332 and K.457. However, it is impossible to assess how closely the notation of these passages reflects the subtlety of Mozart's own performance.

While late eighteenth- and early nineteenth-century pianists such as Mozart and Dussek were particularly noted for their *rubato* techniques,[54] others such as Beethoven do not seem to have used it much, if at all. Despite the extensive documentary evidence concerning the latter's playing, there is not a single reference to it. Among nineteenth-century pianists Chopin was the figure who was most frequently noted for the subtlety of his *rubato*. Whereas pianists such as Liszt habitually, if subtly, lingered on individual beats, Chopin adopted a different approach:

> The hand responsible for the accompaniment would keep strict time, while the other hand, singing the melody, would free the essence of the musical thought from all rhythmic fetters, either by lingering hesitantly or by eagerly anticipating the movement with a certain impatient vehemence akin to passionate speech.[55]

Slurs, dots and wedges

The slur had a variety of meanings in eighteenth- and early nineteenth-century keyboard music. Its most common use in the eighteenth century was over a small group of notes (typically two, three, or four in the Baroque and sometimes rather more later in the century). Used in this way,

Ex. 5.5 Saint-Lambert, *Les principes du clavecin*, Chapter 7

A   B   C   D

Ex. 5.6 Rameau, *Pièces de clavecin* (1724)

the slur in keyboard music is analogous to a bow stroke in string music – all of the notes under a slur would be played in a single bow stroke. Its function is more specific than the phrase mark found in nineteenth- and twentieth-century music. John Butt remarks in his study of Bach's notation that the meaning of the slur 'might vary widely according to context, implying accentuation, dynamic shading or a negation of expected pulses'.[56]

In addition to the meanings that it shared with the notation of string and wind music, the slur was also used in keyboard music to indicate the prolongation of certain notes so that they overlapped with those that followed. The effect is described in a number of French sources. Saint-Lambert devotes Chapter 7 of his *Principes du Clavecin* (Paris, 1702)[57] to the slur. Referring to Example 5.5, which uses only notes of the chord of C major, he comments:

> All the notes that the slur encloses are played, and the effect of the slur is that all these notes are held after having been played, even if their value has expired, and they are only released when it is time to release the last note.[58]

He elaborates, explaining that all of the notes ABCD under the slur are held until the last is released. Later in the same chapter he comments that 'the slur is particularly used in preludes and sometimes in other places, but less frequently'.[59] The French, it seems, were particularly keen that their preludes should be played in as sonorous a manner as possible (the preludes of Couperin's *L'Art de toucher* are full of finger substitutions designed to produce a sustained texture). However, the use of slurs to prolong notes was not confined to preludes. In the execution of the two notes making up the *port de voix*, the first note should be held and released shortly before, or with the second (Ex. 5.6), as Saint-Lambert explains.[60]

Later sources describe the use of the slur to prolong notes, especially in broken chord and arpeggio figuration. C. P. E. Bach refers to the use of this kind of notation as a French characteristic.[61] Louis Adam elaborates:

> When the highest notes form a melody in those places where there is a slur, and if the notes that accompany the melody form a chord, all the notes may then be held under the fingers, as long as the same chord lasts, as follows:[62]

Ex. 5.7 Adam, *Méthode*, p. 152

He goes on to illustrate a similar passage for the left hand. As the damper-raising pedal became increasingly used in the nineteenth century this sort of finger 'super legato' evidently became less popular.[63]

Few articulation markings of any kind are found in the music of the seventeenth century. The biggest problem associated with articulation markings in the eighteenth and early nineteenth centuries is the precise meaning of the dot and wedge (or stroke). The subject is generic to all instruments and is dealt with in the first volume of this series[64] and in other general texts on performance practice. The essence of the interpretation problem is that it is impossible to pinpoint when a difference in meaning between dots and wedges emerged.

A particular problem for the pianist lies in the interpretation of those places where a composer has marked dots or wedges over passages during which the damper-raising pedal is depressed. In some cases, the notation simply reflects what the performer's hands do (see Ex. 2.11). In other instances the composer seems to have a particular effect in mind. Example 5.8 illustrates the point. Here, Beethoven indicates that the sustaining lever or pedal should be depressed for two bars. At the same time, much of the left-hand part has dots placed beneath it. With the pedal sustained, it is impossible for the dampers to fall back onto the strings, however quickly the

Ex. 5.8 Beethoven, Sonata, Op. 53, last movement, bars 55–6

notes are released. However, the composer's principal intention was probably not that these notes should be shortened, but that they should each
receive a sharp accent: in Beethoven's autograph the markings beneath the
notes are mostly very bold, emphatic and wedge-shaped, rather than light,
delicate staccato dots.

Spread chords

Chord spreading, or arpeggiation, is an important aspect of harpsichord and early piano playing (see also Chapter 7). C. P. E. Bach summed up
some of the chief benefits of the practice when he wrote:

> The keyboard lacks the power to sustain long notes and to
> decrease and increase the volume of a tone ... The conditions
> make it no small task to give a singing performance of an adagio
> without creating too much empty space and a consequent
> monotony due to lack of sonority ... The deficiences of the key-
> board can be concealed under various expedients such as broken
> chords.[65]

The technique is discussed in many eighteenth-century tutors and in a
number from the early nineteenth – its importance is underlined in Czerny's
tutor, in which two pages are devoted to the subject.[66]

As with so many other aspects of performance, the extent to which early
keyboard players applied the convention when there were no markings in
the score is unclear. A study of the most comprehensively notated works
provides some clues: the experience of this author is that there are many

Ex. 5.9 Couperin, *L'Art de toucher le clavecin*

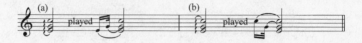

Ex. 5.10 Türk, *Klavierschule* (1789), Chapter 4

Ex. 5.11 Spread chord notation used by Mozart

places in music of the period discussed in this volume where chords should be spread, even where no indication is given in the score.

Spread chords were notated in several different ways in the eighteenth century. In French harpsichord music upwards and downwards arpeggiation were distinguished (Ex. 5.9 a and b). Equivalent symbols are also found in sources such as Rameau's *Pièces de clavecin* (1724), C. P. E. Bach's *Versuch* and Marpurg's *Anleitung*. Türk includes a range of abbreviation symbols in his *Klavierschule* and comments that all of the notes of a chord should be held down until the last one is released, with the exception of the last part of Ex. 5.10. In this instance the first three notes are released and only the main note held.[67] He also notes that, although upwards and downwards arpeggios are both notated, the use of the latter is unusual: it seems that from the late eighteenth century onwards, upward arpeggios were the only sort generally used. Mozart used yet another type of notation for arpeggiated chords (Ex. 5.11).

In addition to the notes of the chords themselves, acciaccaturas were sometimes added, particularly in the Baroque (see Exx. 7.4 and 7.5). As with other ornaments, performers have to decide whether to begin to play an arpeggiated chord on, or before, the beat. While some argue for pre-beat performance, most modern writers assume that the on-beat realisations found in almost all eighteenth-century tutors suggest that the spread should begin on the beat. However, the emergence of a modern practice does seem to be evident in Milchmeyer's tutor of 1797, in which pre-beat performance is notated.[68]

The performance of prolonged arpeggiated passages in the music of Bach, Handel and their contemporaries is discussed in the notation section of Chapter 2.

6   Case studies

Within the confines of a single chapter it is not possible to deal with all of the performance-related aspects of the following works, or groups of works. Taken together, however, these examples demonstrate something of the range and detail of the issues involved in creating historically informed performances.

Most of the material of this chapter is equally applicable to similar parts of the repertory. In some cases, however, the works have been chosen deliberately to demonstrate some more specific points – Mozart's use of the pedalboard, for example. In almost every case there is some comment on the reliability of past and current editions, as well as a discussion about appropriate instruments – important starting points for any historically informed performance.

Louis Couperin's suites

Louis Couperin was born *c.* 1626 at Chaumes. In 1650 Chambonnières met him and persuaded him to move to Paris, where he made a living as a string and keyboard player. In 1653 he became organist at the church of Saint-Gervais, a post that he held until his death in 1661. A small amount of string chamber music by him survives along with some organ music; but it is as a composer for the harpsichord that he is currently best known. Despite the fact that well over 100 harpsichord pieces by him survive, very little is known about their chronology.

Sources and editions

Louis Couperin died before it was customary for keyboard players in Paris to publish their music. His works survive only in manuscript and until fairly recently the Bauyn manuscript was thought to be the only main source of any significance for Louis Couperin's music. This manuscript is an impressive collection of keyboard works by Couperin, Chambonnières and others dating from the last quarter of the seventeenth century. It is now in the Bibliothèque Nationale, Paris and has been reproduced in facsimile by Minkoff, Geneva (1977). Both Brunold's edition of Louis Couperin's music (1936) and its revision by Dart (1959) were based on this source. More recently other sources of Couperin's music have become known. In 1968 an important late seventeenth-century source came to light – the so-called Parville manuscript – prompting Alan Curtis to bring out his edition (Le Pupitre, 1970) which, although it does not contain all of Couperin's harpsichord works, includes some that had not previously been published. In 1985 Brunold's edition was again updated, this time by Davitt Moroney (L'Oiseau Lyre) in a volume that draws on all of the available early sources and includes extensive notes on their differences. There is also a substantial introduction that includes detailed comments on a variety of performance issues.

Instruments

While much of the eighteenth-century French harpsichord repertory is appropriately played on a double-manual instrument by Blanchet or one of his contemporaries, Louis Couperin's music demands a less sonorous, earlier sound. Although little is known about mid-seventeenth-century French harpsichord making it is likely that the instruments were more lightly framed than their eighteenth-century counterparts. Double-manual instruments must have existed (Louis Couperin wrote *pièces croisées* for two manuals – see Chapter 4). In addition to harpsichords made in France, Louis Couperin would almost certainly have known some of the Ruckers instruments that had been made for the French market.

The concept of the 'suite'

Referring to the French suite in the seventeenth century, Gustafson has written:

> There is little evidence that composers conceived the suite as a compositional unit, and in fact most did not use the term (or any other) as a generic heading for the tonal groupings of their pieces. Thematic connections among pieces are rare, and some that exist may be mere coincidence. Suites were not copied as a unit from one manuscript to another . . . Musicians compiled their own

Ex. 6.1 Sarabande in C, bars 17–20 (Bauyn MS, fol. 25v)

suites from existing pieces, creating manuscripts that present groups of dances by more than one composer.[1]

Individual dances were grouped together flexibly in the French repertory, and the sources of Louis Couperin's music illustrate the point. The section of the Bauyn manuscript containing Louis Couperin's works begins with fourteen unmeasured preludes in different keys. Thereafter the dance movements are arranged according to key, a process that has in some instances resulted in lengthy groupings. Immediately following the preludes, for example, a set of dances in C major begins with an allemande, four courantes, seven sarabandes and a number of other dances totalling fifteen in all. Compared with this, the groups of pieces in the Parville manuscript have rather fewer dances, although they sometimes include the works of more than one composer.

Given this apparently chaotic state of affairs, how is the performer to arrange a performance? The publications of members of the French harpsichord school are probably the best guide as to how the dances should be arranged. Published sets of dances more often than not begin with a prelude (the composers probably expected that one would be improvised if none was supplied). The usual pattern is for an allemande to follow the prelude and then for there to be one or more courantes. The courante was evidently very popular and where two were performed there is evidence to suggest that the first was played more slowly than the second.[2] A single sarabande generally follows the courante(s) and there is then a collection of lighter dances, usually including a gigue. A tombeau, chaconne, or set of variations sometimes concludes the group. In all, there may be just a few dances – four or five – or many more; but a popular number was in the region of seven or eight.

In addition to the general observations above, there is evidence that performers sometimes inserted works in the tonic major into groups of dances in the minor mode.[3] So, for example, a D major dance may be placed alongside others in D minor.

Ex. 6.2 Sarabande in C, bars 17–20 (Bauyn MS, fol. 10)

The editors of Louis Couperin's music have arranged the preludes and dances in order to produce suites that are suitable for performance. Of the two most recent editions, Curtis's is rather more directive than Moroney's: the latter encourages the performer to make his or her own choices from the groupings on the contents page.

Variants

A number of writers on this period of French harpsichord music point out that there are substantial differences between versions of the same piece in different sources.[4] This situation seems to reflect the fact that there is no single 'best' text of many of these works, but a number of equally acceptable versions. Even within the same source there are discrepancies. Examples 6.1 and 6.2 show two versions of an extract from a sarabande that appears twice in the Bauyn manuscript. Example 6.1 is attributed to Louis Couperin while Example 6.2, from another folio of the manuscript, is attributed to Chambonnières. It is impossible to say which is the 'better' reading.

Rhythmic differences such as those of Examples 6.1 and 6.2 are frequently found in the sources of Couperin's music, as are differences in ornamentation of the same music. Sometimes there is copious ornamentation in one source but not in another while on other occasions two equally ornamented sources do not agree on all of the ornaments, or their placing. Since it seems to have been accepted among performers of the period that two or more different versions of the same piece might legitimately be played, modern performers have plenty of historical authority for exercising latitude in their performances of this repertory.

Unmeasured preludes

A number of recent writers have addressed the questions associated with the performance of French unmeasured preludes. The introduction to

Moroney's edition provides a number of guidelines and the issues are also discussed in journal articles.[5] Colin Tilney has published an anthology of unmeasured preludes with a brief commentary.[6] The following observations contain some of the most important elements of these studies (see also Chapter 5).

Whereas some composers (d'Anglebert, Marchand, Rameau and others) combine different note values and others used measured notation (François Couperin) in their preludes, Louis Couperin uses only one note value – the semibreve. Despite the differences in notation, preludes by all of these composers are written in essentially the same style, and anyone wishing to perform those by Louis Couperin would be well advised to play through some in which the notation is more varied in order to gain a fuller sense of the style. Moroney advises that the closest parallels to Couperin's unmeasured preludes are Froberger's toccatas, which are very similar in musical, if not notational, style to Couperin's preludes.

An essential point to grasp about Louis Couperin's notation is that, although all of the notes appear the same on the page (i.e., they are all semibreves), their function differs. Troeger points out that the notes are used for 'chordal flourishes such as those that often open or close preludes and toccatas; upbeat figures; complex arpeggio patterns . . . delayed bass entries; many ornaments, especially appoggiaturas, acciaccaturas, and rapid conjunct figures; agglomerations of sustained notes; and detailed and/or unorthodox part-writing'.[7] The challenge to the performer in interpreting the notation is to determine the function of each note. The notation itself provides some clues: copiously provided slurs show which notes are to be sustained and therefore usually indicate those notes that are part of chords.[8] Another general point is that the notation is complete, at least in the sense that it requires no additional notes: even the ornaments are written in, either as semibreves, or as ornament symbols.

In addition to semibreves and various long or short slurs, there are some vertical lines in Louis Couperin's notation. According to Moroney, these lines have three different functions. First, in the case of those vertical lines that look like ordinary bar lines, the notes following them should be played as if they came at the beginning of a bar – in other words, they come on a strong beat. This point is related to another, which is that underlying the rhythmically imprecise notation there is some sense of metre, even though the preludes should clearly be played in a declamatory rather than strictly rhythmical way. The second type of vertical stroke occurs directly above or below a note and seems to imply an accent. Thirdly, two vertically aligned notes sometimes have a vertical stroke placed between them, indicating that they should be played simultaneously, as opposed to the usual manner in which these preludes proceed, with one note following another.

J. S. Bach: French Overture

Bach's *Ouverture nach Französischer Art* (*Overture in the French style*) was published with the *Italian Concerto* in 1735. The two works form the second part of his *Clavier-Übung*, a large compendium of keyboard styles that Bach published in the last two decades of his life, including the six partitas, the so-called 'Organ Mass' and the 'Goldberg Variations'.

The *Ouverture*, like a number of similarly titled works, is in fact a complete suite, the first movement of which is a French overture. While the whole work is ostensibly written in the French style it contains both Italianate and Germanic features. The Overture (first movement), for example, although written in the structure of a French overture has ritornello features (deriving from the Italian concerto style) in its fast section. Some of the dances, especially the Sarabande, are far more contrapuntal than any by French composers, reflecting Bach's German heritage. There is also a 'squareness' about the phrase structure of many of the dances that is not found in 'real' French music. These stylistic features are important considerations in determining the extent to which French performance conventions are appropriate to the work.

Sources and editions

The earliest source of the work, a copy in the hand of Anna Magdalena Bach, is in C minor (BWV 831a). Another copy of this version exists which contains more extensive ornamentation. It was made by the Dortmund organist Preller and probably dates from the middle of the century. It is uncertain why Bach transposed the piece into B minor for the first edition of 1735, although it may have been to emphasise the difference between the French and Italian styles (the *Italian Concerto* is in F major). The first edition was not very carefully prepared for publication and Bach made a number of corrections to it in a copy of which there is a modern fac-simile.[9] A second, improved, printed edition appeared in 1736.

The *French Overture* has not been so popular as some of Bach's other key-board music (such as the '48') and consequently has appeared in fewer modern editions. It was part of the nineteenth-century *Gesamtausgabe* – the complete edition published by Breitkopf & Härtel, which achieved high standards of editing for its time and is currently available in a photo-repro-duction by Dover Publications. Good modern editions have been produced by Henle and Peters, both of which have added (modern-style) fingering. The most authoritative edition is published by Bärenreiter (1977) and is part of the *Neue Bach-Ausgabe*.

Almost all of the editions mentioned in the previous paragraph are of the B minor version, BWV 831. The C minor version BWV 831a was published in 1935 by Schott and is also included in the same volume as the *Italian Concerto* and B minor version of the *French Overture* in the Bärenreiter edition.

As well as the editions mentioned above, there is another by Busoni, edited by Petri and published by Peters (*c.* 1946), that illustrates some of the most extreme trends in early twentieth-century performance. This edition contains pedalling, phrase markings and re-written versions of parts of the piece. It would form an interesting item in a piano recital, even if it bears little resemblance to anything that Bach would have played or heard!

Instruments

Recent discussion of Bach's keyboard music has often focussed on the extent to which he used the clavichord and piano, as well as the harpsi-chord.[10] For Part II of the *Clavier-Übung*, however, he was specific in requir-ing a 'harpsichord with two manuals' ('Clavicymbal mit zweyen Manualen').

For some years at the end of the nineteenth century and beginning of the twentieth it was thought that the appropriate harpsichord disposition for Bach's music was an upper manual with an 8' and 4' and a lower manual with a 16' and 8'. This was known as the 'Bach-disposition' and was based on an instrument in Berlin that was mistakenly thought to have belonged to Bach. In fact, not only was the Bach connection false, but the instrument itself was shown to have been altered at some point in its history. Further details of the saga can be found in Russell's and Hubbard's books.[11]

More recently, attention has focussed on Bach's association with the Berlin maker Michael Mietke, chiefly around the year 1719.[12] Strong circumstantial evidence connects Bach with the maker and it is likely that a surviving double-manual harpsichord with two 8's and a 4' by Mietke (its attribution is virtually certain) was known to Bach. It has been copied by a number of modern makers and has come to be regarded by many as the most appropriate instrument for Bach's music.

Mietke's harpsichords have been described as eclectic in their design.[13] They share many important features of Southern German and Italian instruments, chiefly in their construction, which is relatively light, but they also have similarities with seventeenth-century French and eighteenth-century Hamburg harpsichords. Experience of playing a variety of copies suggests that their sound is not as bright as Italian harpsichords, and not as full as French instruments, especially in the bass; but the clarity and evenness of the sound seems to be ideal for the contrapuntal elements of much of Bach's music.

While the two 8's and single 4' Mietke double-manual harpsichord is in many respects very suitable for Bach's music, it should not be thought of exclusively as the 'right' instrument. There is evidence, for example, that some of Mietke's harpsichords had a 16' register.[14] It is also the case that the evidence linking Bach with Mietke dates from relatively early in his career. His later works might more appropriately be played on other German harpsichords.

Rhythmic issues

Controversy has surrounded the different rhythmic notation of the first section (bars 1–20) of the first movement of the *French Overture*. In the earlier, C minor version (BWV 831a) most of the short upbeat figures are written in semiquavers, though not exclusively so: bars 6, 11 and 12 have demisemiquavers in the left hand and in bars 17–19 all of the short-note runs are in demisemiquavers. The use of semiquavers in BWV 831a is in contrast to the later version in B minor (BWV 831), in which all of the short-note runs of the first section are in demisemiquavers. Examples 6.3 and 6.4 illustrate the differences in the opening bars of the two versions.

The controversy concerns the interpretation of the two different

Ex. 6.3 J. S. Bach, *French Overture* (C minor version, BWV 831a), bars 1–4

Ex. 6.4 J. S. Bach, *French Overture*, (B minor version, BWV 831), bars 1–4

Ex. 6.5 J. S. Bach, *French Overture* (C minor version, Preller MS), bars 1–4

notations.[15] One view is that the B minor version, prepared for publication, represents the way in which Bach actually played the rhythms of the earlier C minor version: in other words, the semiquaver notation of the C minor version is rhythmically imprecise.[16] However, a contrary view has been put forward which suggests that the rhythms of the C minor version should be played as they are notated, and that the notation of the B minor version simply represents an alternative version of the work.[17] Relevant to this view is the later copy by Preller of the C minor version which has ornaments added in some of the semiquaver passages, making it impossible to perform them as demisemiquavers (Ex. 6.5). However, although this version of the piece is interesting, it may have no connection with the way in which Bach himself played it.

The debate over the first movement of the *French Overture* has revealed a great deal about the performance of dotted rhythms in the Baroque; but it would be untrue to claim that any consensus yet exists about the precise way in which the versions should be played.

The Baroque practice of *notes inégales*, in which certain notes that are rhythmically identical are played unequally (usually long–short, much less commonly short–long), is extensively written about elsewhere and will not be described in detail here.[18] It seems to have been a more or less universal practice among French musicians, but its application to music written outside of France is more difficult to assess. Some, such as Georg Muffat, advocated it in his French-style works, but the evidence for its use in the music of many composers is open to debate.

There can be little doubt that Bach knew of the *inégales* convention. He heard French-style performances at the court of Celle in his youth and he knew a number of French musicians. He also knew the keyboard works of a number of French composers. Since the title page of Bach's *Clavier-Übung* Part II makes the specific point that BWV 831 is composed 'in the French style' ('nach Französischer Art') we might infer that the composer intended French performance conventions to be used, despite the lack of any indication to that effect in the early editions, and despite the fact that the French style is not wholly convincingly imitated in the music. Modern scholars are divided on the issue. Neumann wrote that 'it will be advisable to limit the use of *inégalité* to French composers . . .'[19] A different view is put forward by Hefling. Speaking of music by non-French composers he writes 'very likely inequality was applied to music of French origin and to works that obviously emulate French style'.[20]

Repeats

Repetition patterns in seventeenth- and eighteenth-century music are not always easy to determine. In the case of those dances with an ornamented *double* it is not always clear whether the repetition pattern is AABBA'A'B'B' or AA'BB', or some other arrangement.[21] In some short dances of the Baroque, each section was repeated three times. Evidently there was a degree of flexibility.[22] However, in pairs of movements such as the Gavottes, Passepieds and Bourrées of the *French Overture*, where a *da capo* of the first dance is played after the second, the repeats seem normally to have been observed in the *da capo*. In other words the overall form of each pair of dances was probably AABBCCDDAABB. It is probable that the practice of missing out the *da capo* repeats only gained ground in the late eighteenth century.[23]

The performance of a *petite reprise* – a (probably ornamented) *piano* repetition of the last few bars of a dance movement following the second playing of the second half – was a common feature of French harpsichord music which was sometimes, but not always, notated. Very occasionally there is evidence of the practice in Bach's music. The written-out ornamented version of the last bars in the Air of the E minor Partita, BWV 830 is an example. Although there is no indication of the practice in the French Overture, a *petite reprise* might, for example, be appropriate at the end of the last playing of Bourrée I.

Haydn: Sonata in C minor, Hob.XVI:20

The C minor Sonata is seen by most commentators as a work of particular importance among Haydn's keyboard works. Its intensity mirrors that of the *Sturm und Drang* symphonies of the early 1770s, a period during which Haydn's style developed significantly in a number of genres.

Sources and editions

The earliest source for the sonata is an autograph fragment dated 1771. At some time between the date of this source and the first edition of 1780 Haydn finished the work, but the precise date of its completion remains uncertain. The C minor Sonata was published as the sixth of a set for 'Clavicembalo o Forte Piano' that included Hob.XX:35–9.

Of the editions currently available, Christa Landon's (Wiener Urtext) and Georg Feder's (Henle) are the best. Dover Publications have issued a photoreproduction of the early complete edition by Breitkopf & Härtel which, for its time, was edited to high standards. Another readily available edition is that of Martienssen (Peters), but this is not to be recommended on account of its large number of unacknowledged editorial interventions. Howard Ferguson's edition for the Associated Board of some of Haydn's sonatas is reliable, but unfortunately does not include the C minor Sonata under discussion here.

Instruments

Until recently it was thought that Haydn's C minor Sonata was written for the piano, on account of its numerous dynamic markings and the designation 'Sonata per il Clavicembalo o Forte Piano' on the title page of the first edition. However, the most relevant recent studies suggest other-

wise.[24] The earliest reference to a piano in documents relating to Haydn is
contained in a letter of his dated 26 October 1788. Some have tried to infer
that there was a piano at Esterháza because of a receipt dated 3 March 1781
referring to a visit made by the Viennese piano maker Anton Walter.
However, the receipt was for repairing 'Clavier und Flügel Instrumenten'
and there is no mention of a piano.[25] Another reference notes a performance
on a piano at a concert in Esterháza in 1773, but the source was written ten
years after the event by an individual who was not a musician.[26] Such sources
are notoriously unreliable in details concerning musical instruments and
since this account is out of step with most of what is known about the availability of pianos in the area, it cannot be relied upon.

Pianos were almost certainly not made in Vienna before the 1780s. A very
small number of sources refer to isolated performances on pianos in the
1760s and 1770s. These instruments were probably (in one case definitely)
imported instruments. However, by far the most common keyboard instruments in use in the city at that time were harpsichords (usually single-
manuals, although double-manuals were known) and clavichords.[27]

Maunder has suggested that the C minor Sonata might originally have
been written for a double-manual harpsichord. The dynamics would indeed
be realisable on such an instrument, but it seems much more likely that the
sonata was intended for the clavichord.

Articulation

General comments regarding articulation in late eighteenth-
century keyboard music will be found in Chapters 4 and 5. The present discussion is confined to the specific issue of the meaning of dots and strokes
(or wedges) in Haydn's music. This is particularly important in the case of
Haydn's C minor Sonata, in which there are many strokes, rather than dots –
a feature that is acknowledged in the modern scholarly editions of Landon
and Feder. Whether there is any difference in the meaning of these two signs,
and whether they are used with any degree of consistency has been a hotly
debated subject in relation to the music of J. S. Bach, Mozart and Beethoven,
among others.[28] Their meaning in Haydn's music has recently been reviewed
in detail by Harrison.[29]

From his detailed study of the manuscript and printed sources of Haydn's
music Harrison makes a number of observations about Haydn's use of

strokes and dots. In the earliest works, only the stroke is used. In works written after 1766 dots begin to be used and they occur with increasing frequency in the later works, all the time alongside strokes. Harrison argues that Haydn's autograph markings are very careful, but that the engravers who prepared the first editions did not always follow Haydn's wishes.

In the period of the C minor Sonata Harrison convincingly demonstrates that the stroke is used to indicate staccato. The dot, when it occurs, means the same as *portato*, or the *Tragen der Töne*, a clavichord effect in which the notes are not actually shortened, but are each given an added pressure of the fingers, so that they are given a slight emphasis (see Chapter 4).

The numerous strokes that are found in the C minor Sonata, therefore, are indications to shorten the notes over which they occur. They do not indicate the kind of accent that the symbol later came to imply.

Mozart: Piano Concerto in C major, K.467

The Concerto was composed during one of Mozart's busiest periods as a pianist and composer. The completion of his previous major work, the Concerto in D minor, K.466, was noted in his own list of works on 10 February 1785 and was performed on the following day. The autograph of the C major Concerto, K.467 is headed 'February 1785': work was presumably begun after he had finished and performed K.466 and the completed concerto was entered in the composer's list of works on 9 March 1785. The first performance took place with the composer at the keyboard on the following day at one of a series of concerts that he organised.

Sources and editions

The chief source of the work is the composer's autograph manuscript, currently in the Pierpont Morgan Library, New York and reproduced in facsimile by Dover Publications. The haste with which Mozart prepared the autograph in February and early March of 1785 is evident in the way in which the music is written on the page and in the numerous shorthand instructions used by the composer, some of which create difficulties of interpretation (see below). Although plenty of performance detail was included in the orchestral parts, there is less in the keyboard part – some articulation, but very few dynamics. No original cadenzas survive. The first edition dates from 1800, nine years after the composer's death. It was based on the autograph and provides little additional information.

The mid-nineteenth-century complete edition, published by Breitkopf & Härtel, is one of the cheapest available in its photo-reproduced form by Dover Publications. However, it is one of the poorer volumes of the old complete edition, characterised by numerous editorial interventions. The aim of the editor was evidently to ensure as legato a performance as possible, hence the lengthy slurs over semiquaver passages. Mozart's careful articulation markings, where they exist in the piano part, are changed in favour of slurs over the barline and other features entirely uncharacteristic of the composer.

There are two readily available modern scores that are generally reliable and faithful to Mozart's original. Friedrich Blume's edition for Eulenburg first appeared in 1934. An introduction was added by Denis Matthews in 1972 which includes some useful suggestions for lead-ins (see below). The second modern score is from the *Neue Mozart-Ausgabe* (*NMA*). Like the Eulenburg edition, it is based on the autograph. Neither the Eulenburg edition nor the *NMA* includes detailed textual comments (although they may be found in the relevant critical commentary for the *NMA*, published separately, in German).

Instruments

Despite the designation 'cembalo' in the score, there is no doubt that Mozart intended the work to be played on the piano. At some time during the previous few years he had acquired a piano by the Viennese maker Anton Walter and it must have been this instrument that he used for concerts in 1785. Referring to the previous month's activities, his father wrote to Wolfgang's sister on 12 March 1785 that 'your brother's fortepiano has been taken at least a dozen times to the theatre or to some other house'.[30] The instrument is now in the Internationale Stiftung Mozarteum in Salzburg and has been copied by a number of modern makers. Whether this instrument is now exactly as it was when it was played by Mozart has recently been cast into doubt: scholars have found evidence that the action has been altered.[31]

In the letter of 12 March 1785 Leopold Mozart also commented that Wolfgang 'has had a large fortepiano pedal made, which stands under the instrument and is about two feet longer and extremely heavy'.[32] Leopold was referring to a separate instrument, with its own strings and action, which

Ex. 6.6 Mozart, Concerto in D minor, K. 466, first movement, bars 88–91

was played with the feet, like an organ pedalboard. The instrument no longer survives, but it is well documented[33] and was used in the concert at which Mozart premiered K.467: an announcement was published informing the public that 'not only a new, just finished Forte piano Concerto will be played by him, but also an especially large Forte piano pedal will be used by him in improvising'.[34]

Since the pedalboard was presumably in place while Mozart played the concerto we can assume that he used it for the work's first performance. Yet there is no indication in the score for the notes that he played with his feet. In fact, there is only one passage in all of Mozart's piano music that contains notes specifically intended for the pedalboard: bars 88–90 of the first movement of the Concerto in D minor, K.466 (Ex. 6.6). So what might Mozart have played with his feet in the C major Concerto, K.467? From the available accounts of Mozart's use of the instrument it appears that the pedalboard was particularly suited to works in improvisatory styles – fantasias and the like. The cadenzas therefore seem appropriate places for its use. One particular feature of Mozart's autograph score is also suggestive as far as the pedalboard is concerned. The two staves of the piano part are written immediately above the stave for the stringed bass instruments (the bottom line of the score), so that the cello and bass line can conveniently be read as the pedal part of an organ score. Of course, only very few modern performers will have the opportunity to experiment with a pedalboard for the performance of this concerto, but an understanding of its possible use in the work might lead to some judicious octave doublings in the left-hand part from time to time.

Cadenzas and lead-ins

No cadenzas by Mozart survive for K.467, yet clearly they are required. The customary pause over a second-inversion chord followed by a perfect cadence into the tonic occurs at bar 396 of the first movement and at bar 424 of the last movement. In 1801 P. K. Hoffmann published some cadenzas for the concerto, but already by that date the piano style had changed, and the cadenzas are somewhat long and harmonically more adventurous than Mozart would probably have wanted. Later in the nine-teenth century Busoni wrote cadenzas for many of Mozart's concertos, including K.467, which are lengthy and more harmonically extreme than Hoffmann's, and similarly over-blown cadenzas followed in the twentieth century by Schnittke and others. Kempff's cadenzas for K.467 are rather more economical, but the best modern examples in print are probably those of Paul Badura-Skoda (Bärenreiter).

In addition to the main cadenzas of the outer movements, there are several more occasions for brief improvisatory lead-ins by the soloist: bar 79 of the first movement and bars 20 and 177 of the last movement. The sugges-tions by Denis Matthews in the introduction to the Eulenburg score are brief and stylish, as are Badura-Skoda's, published with his cadenzas.

Some notational features

It has been acknowledged by many modern scholars that Mozart sketched, rather than wrote out in full, some sections of the piano parts of his concertos – not surprising in view of the haste with which the works were prepared for their first performances. The issue is discussed in Eva and Paul Badura-Skoda's *Interpreting Mozart on the keyboard*.[35] Mozart probably intended some additional figuration to be supplied, for example, where a passage of small note values comes to a sudden halt and is followed by a large interval. Bar 380 of the first movement of K.467 has been identified by a number of scholars and performers as one of these places and has therefore been 'filled in' by the editor of the *NMA*. Levin has suggested that bars 58–9 of the slow movement should be elaborated. He has also raised the possibil-ity of substituting broken octaves in the right-hand part for the octave quaver passages in bars 143–4, 149–50, 302, 304–6, 394–5 and 400–1 of the last movement.[36]

One of the most vexing notational issues in K.467 is the length of dotted notes in the slow movement. In bar 24, for example, at the beginning of one of the best-known of Mozart's themes, it is customary for the small notes following the doubly-dotted crotchets to be printed *after* the last of the triplet quavers in the left-hand part (Ex. 6.7). Almost all performers play the theme in this way. But how can we be certain that Mozart did not intend

Ex. 6.7 Mozart, Concerto in C, K.467, second movement, bars 24–5

the right-hand semiquavers in these bars to be played at the same time as the last triplet notes of the left-hand part? To do so would be to follow a very common convention of notation for the time (see Chapter 2).

The alignment of the right-hand semiquavers relative to the left-hand triplets is unclear in the autograph, because Mozart has used a shorthand notation for the triplets. However, an important clue to the performance of the theme at bar 24 can be found in the notation of other long–short rhythms in the movement. In bars 38, 43, 63, etc. (including the final melodic idea in bars 99ff.) dotted quavers are followed by semiquavers: this is the most frequently used long–short rhythmic notation of the movement. In the total absence, anywhere in the movement, of a triplet crotchet plus quaver grouping, we might assume, therefore, that the dotted-quaver-plus-semiquaver rhythm can be played as a triplet, in what might be considered the usual way for the eighteenth century. However, what are we to make of the dotted crotchet and quaver notation of bars 30 and 32 (identically notated at the return of this idea at bars 94 and 96)? Mozart seems to have made a point of writing this melodic idea differently from that of bar 24, and considering the consistency with which the two notations are used we might assume that he intended the rhythms to be performed differently. Perhaps bars 30 and 32 are *real* quavers (rather than triplets).

Continuo

As with other concertos of the time, it seems that the soloist should supply a continuo part during the orchestral tuttis. Clearly, this would have been improvised by the composer in his performances of the work, although there is no notation of a continuo part in the score. However, there are several places in which the first few bass notes of the tutti are written in the piano part, followed by the customary shorthand 'col basso' indicating that the pianist should follow the orchestral bass part (see Chapter 7).

Beethoven: Sonata in D major, Op. 10, No. 3

The sonata was probably composed in the years 1795–8, during which Beethoven was establishing himself as a pianist and composer. He had arrived in Vienna towards the end of 1792, but his public performing career was only established in 1795, when he played his early piano concertos in Vienna. Success in the Austrian capital was followed in 1796 by concerts in Prague, Dresden, Berlin, Budapest and other nearby towns and cities. On his return to Vienna he continued to work on the composition and publication of his early works. Op. 10, No. 3 was published in Vienna in 1798.

Sources and editions

The autograph of the sonata is lost and the only significant source for the work is the first edition, published under the composer's supervision in Vienna.

There are numerous modern editions of Beethoven's sonatas from which to choose. They fall into three main categories. In the first are those editions with copious additions of phrasing, pedalling, fingering, etc. indicated by markings that are not necessarily distinguishable from the composer's own. The Associated Board's edition by Tovey and Craxton is probably the most readily available example.

A second group of editions are those in which editorial interventions are more easily distinguishable from the composer's markings. This approach has been followed by many, if not most, recent editors. Typically, the majority of details in the score follow the most important early sources carefully, although the occasional incorporation of markings deriving from, for example, Czerny's evidence, is not acknowledged. These editions also tend to have copious editorial fingerings, sometimes, but not always, distinguished from the composer's own. Examples of this approach will be found in the editions by Schenker, revised by Ratz (Vienna Urtext, Universal), Pauer, revised by Martienssen (Peters – Pauer's name does not appear in the more recent issues), and Wallner, with fingering by Hansen (Henle). An edition that has rather more editorial suggestions for performance, but in which editorial markings are clearly distinguished from the composer's, is Arrau's (Henry Litolff/Peters).

The third type of edition is unencumbered by editorial suggestions. The nineteenth-century complete edition (reproduced in a modern miniature score) is 'clean', as is the edition by Schmidt which forms part of the new complete edition, published by Henle (general editor, Joseph Schmidt-Görg).

Instruments

Beethoven would have had an opportunity to play a variety of pianos on his travels in the 1790s and in Vienna itself there were instruments by foreign makers. Haydn owned an English piano by Longman and Broderip, Hummel performed on an English grand at a concert on 12 March 1794, and other English pianos are mentioned in the Viennese press.[37] In 1803 Beethoven received the gift of a piano from the French maker Erard and further gifts followed, notably of a Broadwood piano that arrived in Vienna in 1818. Nevertheless, despite Beethoven's experience of a wide range of pianos, Newman has made a strong case for the composer's preference for Viennese pianos throughout his life.[38]

In the second half of the 1790s, the period most immediately relevant to Op. 10, No. 3, Beethoven was particularly associated with the piano makers Nannette Streicher and Anton Walter. On 19 November 1796 he wrote to his friend Johann Andreas Streicher (Nannette's husband) thanking him for sending a piano to Pressburg in Hungary (present-day Bratislava in Slovakia) for a concert.[39] In 1801, when Czerny first visited Beethoven he noticed a Walter piano in the composer's room and the correspondence between the composer and piano maker is evidence of their business relationship.[40]

The most appropriate instrument for Op. 10, No. 3 is a Streicher or a Walter, although it is likely that Beethoven played the work on a number of other types of piano.

'Missing' notes

The notation of Op. 10, No. 3 is peculiar in that there are a few places where notes appear to be 'missing': in other words, there are notes that look as if they should obviously be included, but which are not found in the first edition. In modern editions these notes have generally been added in small notes, in brackets, or by some other means that distinguishes them from the notes included in the first edition. The first instances are the bottom E in bar 15 and the top F♯ in bar 22 of the first movement. Other instances follow later in the movement, such as the 'missing' bass notes of bars 271–2. The problem is not unique to Op. 10, No. 3 – there is no top G♭ in bar 128 of the first movement of Op. 10, No. 1, for example – but the concentration of 'missing' notes is at its greatest in Op. 10, No. 3.

The reason for this notational peculiarity has to do with the compass of pianos at the end of the eighteenth century. The 'normal' compass of grand pianos in Vienna and the surrounding regions was 5 octaves, from FF to f³. However, makers of keyboard instruments in both Austria and Germany had for some time included additional notes in the treble – up to g³ or a³ – and they were doing so with increasing frequency in the 1790s. Beethoven would undoubtedly have been familiar with instruments that had sufficient notes to allow the performance of the treble 'missing' notes in Op. 10, No. 3. They were presumably omitted from the first edition for commercial reasons, however, because the ownership of pianos with notes above f³ was not sufficiently widespread in Austria at the time.

The 'missing' notes in the bass are more difficult to explain. These notes could have been played on some of the more up-to-date English instruments of the time (whose extended bass compass had become popular in London in the mid 1790s), but not on any continental pianos that are known. Given the nature of the notation (which is unusual), we should probably assume that Beethoven intended these 'missing' bass notes to be played. But precisely which instruments he had in mind remains a mystery.[41]

Pedalling[42]

There are no markings for pedals in Op. 10, No. 3. In fact, there are no pedal markings in Beethoven's published music before 1801. However, this does not mean that he only began to use the damper-raising and other devices in that year. There are very brief indications for the use of the knee levers (the standard mechanism for raising the dampers and for other devices on 'Viennese' pianos at the time) in the 'Kafka' sketchbook (c. 1790–2) and early sources of the Concertos Opp. 15 and 19 (c. 1795). His pupil Czerny also remarked that 'BEETHOVEN ... employed it [the damper-raising device] in the performance of his pianoforte works much more frequently than we find it indicated in those compositions.'[43] Czerny's evidence cannot relate to the 1790s, because he only later met Beethoven; but it is a general indication of the way in which the composer treated his own scores.

Having established that Beethoven may have used knee levers or pedals in Op. 10, No. 3, we cannot easily imagine where he may have done so. One of his most characteristic uses of the damper-raising device in works published around this time is in extended passages, often through changes in harmony, such as the first movement of Op. 27, No. 2 and the beginning of the final movement of Op. 53 (the 'Waldstein'). Czerny noted that Beethoven adopted a similar approach in the performance of the slow movement of his 3rd Piano Concerto: 'Beethoven (who publicly played this Concerto in 1803) continued the pedal during the entire theme.'[44] It is conceivable that Beethoven played passages such as bars 105–13 of the first movement, or the beginning or end of the slow movement of Op. 10, No. 3 in this way, although had he done so Czerny would probably have recorded the fact.

Beethoven sometimes used the damper-raising pedal when the left-hand accompaniment spanned more than an octave – a very popular texture with early pianist/composers. The passage beginning in bar 23 of the first movement has some of these characteristics and might benefit from the use of the damper-raising lever or pedal. Beethoven also notated the damper-raising lever or pedal for emphasis, or for connecting one section of music to another. The notes under the pauses in bars 4, 22, 132, etc. of the first movement serve both purposes and might therefore be pedalled, as might the last chords of the first movement. We cannot rule out the possibility that Beethoven used the pedal as modern pianists do, for creating legato and a sonorous effect, especially in the slow movement. However, Czerny's remarks should make us cautious: '[Beethoven] understood remarkably well how to connect full chords to each other without the use of the pedal.'[45]

At the time of the publication of Op. 10, No. 3 the usual soft pedal on Viennese pianos was the moderator, for which there is no evidence of Beethoven's use. However, he seems to have been one of the most frequent users of the *una corda* pedal, once it became established on Viennese pianos in the early years of the nineteenth century. If he did use it in later performances of Op. 10, No. 3, the first movement, bars 105–13 and the beginning and end of the slow movement are likely places.

Chopin: Nocturne in E♭, Op. 9, No. 2

Having been born, brought up and taught to play the piano in Warsaw, Chopin left the city in 1830, at the age of twenty, and travelled to Vienna. After a few months in the city he travelled through Germany and in 1831 settled in Paris, by then the home of Liszt and a number of other piano virtuosi. Chopin occasionally played in public, especially during his earlier years in Paris, but gained a reputation as a much more private, less flamboyant musician than Liszt. Chopin's Nocturne, Op. 9, No. 2, published in 1832, typifies the introverted side of Chopin's style that became his hallmark.

Sources and editions

The source history of Chopin's music is often complex. A useful and easily accessible summary of some of the problems will be found in Samson's *Chopin*.[46] Briefly, there were many stages of composition with Chopin, who continued to revise works up to, and after, publication. He arranged for simultaneous publication of his works in France, Germany and England, a situation that led to discrepancies in early sources. So for any composition there may be sketches, autographs, copies made by copyists for certain publishers, proof copies and more than one first edition. In addition, Chopin was in the habit of making annotations to copies belonging to his pupils, so that the text continued to develop after publication. The Nocturne, Op. 9, No. 2 is one of Chopin's works with the greatest number of variants, notably in the embellishments of the right-hand part and in versions of the closing bars of the piece.

There are numerous editions of Chopin's nocturnes, of which only a few can be mentioned here. Some of those that have been widely used in the past contain extensive interventions by their respective editors so that it is impossible to discover which performance directions were made by the composer. Among these are Klindworth's (Augener) and Fielden's (Associated Board) editions. Other editions deviate from the early sources because they include details passed on to pupils by Chopin during lessons. Mikuli's edition (Schirmer) is based on the editor's lessons with the composer while Ganche's edition relies on the markings made by Chopin on music belonging to another pupil, Jane Stirling.

Modern 'scholarly' editions take different approaches to the variety of source material. The Polish 'Paderewski' edition is based on early sources, but the choice of the main source for each work has been criticised.[47] Theopold's edition (Henle) uses the earlier sources more convincingly, but largely disregards Chopin's later amendments. Ekier, on the other hand, is so concerned to include as much information as possible about the various 'authentic' versions that both of his editions print Op. 9, No. 2 twice. In each case, the first version of the work is based on the earliest sources whereas the second version contains information from the scores of a number of Chopin's pupils. Ekier's first edition of the nocturnes is part of the Wiener Urtext Edition (Universal) and was published in 1980. His second edition, which contains additional source information to his 1980 edition, is part of the Polish National Edition (not to be confused with the 'Paderewski' Polish edition) of which Ekier himself is the general editor. The latter is the most informative of all the scholarly editions.

Different versions of Op. 9, No. 2

Among the most significant amendments made by Chopin in his pupils' copies were the additions of new or different passages of melodic decoration.[48] So, for example, the quaver upbeat of the early editions at the end of bar 4 became a run of ten or thirteen notes, depending on the source. Similarly, the first half of bar 14 exists in two heavily ornamented versions. In one source the embellishments of the second beat of bar 16 were begun during the first beat and included many more notes. Further embellishments of a similar nature are documented.

The other major differences in the versions recorded by Chopin's pupils concern the end of the nocturne. In one variant version the work is extended by one bar with the inclusion of a 5-octave arpeggio of E♭. In another, there are two extra bars, again with a 5-octave arpeggio and, this time, with the addition of some extra chords.

Performers who wish to experiment with different versions of this nocturne can do so with ease from the information provided in Ekier's editions. However, they would do well to heed his advice: 'a careful selection must be made from the Chopin variants which appear in different teaching copies; certainly they should not all be played in their entirety'.[49]

The left-hand part

Contrary to the way in which the nocturne is often played nowadays, Chopin wanted the left-hand part to be played steadily, without any
change to the metre (except in places such as bars 10 and 12 where *poco rit.*
and *poco rallent.* occur). Von Lenz, one of his pupils, stressed the importance
of this: 'the bass to be practised first by itself, divided between the two hands
... once the bass part is mastered – with two hands – with a full but piano
sonority and in strict time, maintaining an absolutely steady allegretto
movement ... then the left hand can be trusted with the accompaniment
played that way and the tenor invited to sing his part in the upper voice'.[50]
Similar comments about Chopin's time-keeping were made by others of his
pupils. Mikuli, for example, remarked that 'in keeping time Chopin was
inexorable, and some readers will be surprised to learn that the metronome
never left his piano'.[51]

Von Lenz's remarks about this nocturne also included a somewhat enig-
matic comment to the effect that the left-hand part 'should sound like a
chorus of guitars'.[52] Perhaps by this he was suggesting that the chords should
be slightly arpeggiated.

Rubato

Mikuli discussed Chopin's metronomic playing in the context of his
tempo rubato: 'even in his much maligned tempo rubato, the hand respon-
sible for the accompaniment would keep strict time, while the other hand,
singing the melody, would free the essence of the musical thought from all
rhythmic fetters, either by lingering hesitantly or by eagerly anticipating the
movement with a certain impatient vehemence akin to passionate speech'.[53]
In a work with such an uncomplicated melody-plus-accompaniment
texture as Op. 9, No. 2 there is ample opportunity for this sort of *rubato*. But
should it be applied throughout, or should it be confined to the passage
beginning in bar 26, where the direction *poco rubato* occurs? At the very
least, the effect should presumably be particularly noticeable at bar 26,
where it is specifically called for; but that need not completely rule out its use
elsewhere. Indeed, two of the amendments made in a copy for one of
Chopin's pupils suggest that it may be appropriate elsewhere in the movement. For Mikuli, Chopin indicated the delayed playing of the third quaver

(and all subsequent notes until the third beat) of bar 8. He similarly indicated the late playing of the third quaver of bar 16.

Performance of embellished passages

In 1913 Kleczynski, who had sought out information from a number of Chopin's pupils, wrote that 'Chopin differed, in his manner of using arabesques and parenthetical ornamentations, from the usual manner of his time, which was to dwell upon such passages and to endue them with importance.'[54] To illustrate his point he chose, among other examples, bars 16 and 24 from Op. 9, No. 2 where, he said, the ornamental passages should begin slowly and accelerate to their conclusions. Von Lenz put it rather differently: 'they should sound as though improvised, the result not of studying exercises but of your sheer mastery of the instrument'.[55] Chopin's fingerings, included in the modern scholarly editions, suggest a lightness in some of these passages, with their use of the weaker fingers 4 and 5 on successive notes.

7   Continuo realisation

The brief discussion of continuo playing in this chapter focusses mainly on instrumentation, style and recitative accompaniment. Other matters are dealt with in detail elsewhere, especially in the studies of F. T. Arnold and Peter Williams.[1] Arnold's study, first published in 1931, contains remarkably detailed coverage of the seventeenth- and eighteenth-century sources and remains an important survey of the subject, although the author does not fully represent the variety of continuo practice that existed in the Baroque. Peter Williams' more practically oriented work is an extremely useful manual for the performer. In addition to Arnold and Williams, a number of specialist studies exist[2] along with translations of some of the most important early treatises and the practical figured-bass exercises of composers such as Bach and Handel.[3]

A study of figured-bass notation itself lies outside the scope of this chapter, but a brief summary is given here, by way of introduction. There are several layers of complexity attaching to the system of symbols that comprises a figured-bass part. The fundamentals are easy to grasp: a figure placed above or below a bass note denotes the interval above the note that should be played. A figure 6 above or below a bass note therefore implies the performance of a note an interval of a sixth above the bass. Except in the very earliest figured basses, only the figures 1–9 are generally used, so performers must choose in which octave they play an interval. A figure 6 above or below a note may therefore be performed as a sixth or as a thirteenth, depending on the performer's choice. Within the system there are abbreviations with which performers need to be familiar. A single figure (or no figure) will generally imply a fuller chord. So, a figure 6 on its own generally implies the addition of the third of the chord, and perhaps other notes as well. Useful discussions of chord abbreviations are found in both Arnold and Williams.[4]

There are some inconsistencies within the notation. Whereas one composer or publisher might use a sharp sign to raise an interval by a semitone, another will use a natural sign in the same circumstance while another still will use a slash through the figure. These slashes through figures can themselves be a source of confusion: they mostly indicate a rise of a semitone, but they are occasionally used to indicate a flattening of an interval by a semitone. Anomalies also exist: a figure 1, for example, may be used to indicate an octave. The correct solution to most of these problems will be obvious to any moderately experienced continuo player, but the notation has the capacity constantly to surprise, so that a careful reading of Arnold, Williams and other sources that discuss the meaning of the figures themselves may save some embarrassment![5]

Instrumentation

The second part of C. P. E. Bach's *Versuch* describes continuo accompaniment comprising the organ, harpsichord, clavichord, or piano, with string bass and includes the often-quoted remark 'the best accompaniment, one which is free of criticism, is a keyboard instrument and a cello'.[6] Undoubtedly, a continuo line played by a cello and keyboard instrument works extremely well, especially for much of the smaller-scale Baroque repertory; but it should not be thought of as the only, or even the normal lineup in either chamber music, or in works for larger forces.

There is ample evidence to suggest that continuo parts of much Baroque chamber music were played by a single instrument. In Italian chamber sonatas of the later seventeenth century the bass line was often played by a stringed bass instrument alone, or by a spinet, or harpsichord.[7] (In Italian instrumental church music, however, the bass line often seems to have been doubled by an organ and melody-bass instrument.) Corelli's Op. 5 Sonatas for violin have occasioned some debate on account of their title page, which specifies 'Violino e violone o cimbalo', but it is now largely accepted that the title page means exactly what it says – 'violin and violone or harpsichord'.[8] Handel appears to have continued the practice of using only one instrument on the bass line in some of his sonatas. 'Of the five solo sonatas by Handel which have some reference to the accompaniment in the autograph title, only the E minor flute Sonata . . . has "Sonata a Travers. E Basso"; the other four appear to indicate harpsichord alone – the recorder Sonatas viii, ix and xi [in g, a and F, HWV 360, 362 and 369] have "Sonata a Flauto e Cembalo", and the violin Sonata in D (xiv [HWV 371]) has "Sonata a Violino e Cembalo. . ."[9] Despite the widespread use of a single instrument on the bass line of chamber works the use of a keyboard instrument in combination with a melody-bass instrument became increasingly popular in chamber sonatas from around 1700 and it can certainly be regarded as the normal arrangement for mid-eighteenth-century music.

More than one chord-playing instrument featured in the performance of the bass lines of many larger-scale Baroque works. Sometimes there were duplicate keyboard instruments, but on other occasions the keyboard instrument was joined by another type of plucked-string instrument. In 1701 Muffat advised that the bass line should be 'ornamented' 'with harpsi-chord, theorbos, harps and similar instruments' if the number of players exceeded 2–3 players per part in a concerto grosso.[10] Quantz stated that there should be an additional harpsichord and theorbo if twelve violins played in an opera pit.[11] Many Baroque concertos have two separate parts for chord-playing instruments, including notable examples such as J. S. Bach's Concerto in A major for harpsichord (BWV 1055), which contains a figured bass part in addition to the solo keyboard part.

The number of continuo instruments used in Baroque opera varied. In England up to the 1720s a single harpsichord seems to have been usual. Thereafter, at least to the mid-1730s, two harpsichords were used, a practice that was evidently common on the continent.[12] Precisely how the labour was divided between two continuo harpsichords is uncertain, although there is evidence that they alternated in dialogue recitative, each singer being accompanied by his or her own harpsichord.[13] Multiple keyboard instru-ments were also used in Handel's oratorios, in which both organ and harpsi-chord featured. The harpsichord seems to have been played throughout these works while the organ was reserved mainly for chorus movements (the organ did not normally play in secco recitatives or in arias). In those works with double choir two organs were sometimes used, one for each choir.[14] Bach's liturgical choral music also seems to have featured the harpsichord and organ. Dreyfus has made a case for playing the two instruments together for a substantial proportion of these works, including recitatives.[15] There is also evidence that Bach used two harpsichords in some non-liturgical vocal works.[16]

Keyboard continuo was usual in vocal and choral music of the second half of the eighteenth century and into the early decades of the nineteenth – the first edition of Beethoven's *Missa Solemnis* (published in 1827) has a fully written-out continuo part for the organ. But for orchestral music in the same period performing practice seems to have varied significantly according to local custom. In 1791 Galeazzi wrote about the arrangements for a concert orchestra in a drawing room: 'with regard to the bass-line instruments, if there are only two, place them near the harpsichord (if there is one)'.[17] Galeazzi was reflecting orchestral practices in parts of Italy and he implies that the harpsichord was not always used. Indeed, it is likely that many performances of symphonies on the continent were given without a keyboard instrument, especially those for smaller orchestra.[18] James Webster has made a persuasive case for the absence of any keyboard continuo in Haydn's symphonies written for performance at Eszterháza: there is no documentary evidence for the presence of a keyboard player and Haydn probably led the performances from the violin.[19] Nevertheless, performances of Classical orchestral works with keyboard continuo are documented. Gassmann played the harpsichord in Viennese concerts in 1763 and a symphony by Rosetti was directed from the keyboard at a Viennese concert in 1783. Leopold Mozart relates how a harpsichord was used by Michael Haydn for a concert made up of instrumental music in 1777 and how Nannerl Mozart accompanied symphonies at a private concert in the following year.[20] In London, Haydn followed local custom by directing concert performances of his later symphonies from the keyboard – even incorporating a short keyboard solo in Symphony no. 98.[21]

The choice of a harpsichord or piano for late eighteenth-century continuo playing must often have depended upon which instrument was available. Many, if not most opera houses, for example, maintained harpsichords and spinets for some time after the piano had become a popular concert instrument – well into the nineteenth century, in fact.[22] However, experience of playing continuo for late eighteenth-century scores shows that the all-or-nothing qualities of the harpsichord do not always sit well with the instrumental textures of the music, especially in slow movements. Koch, writing in 1802, argued for the use of the piano, particularly in smaller rooms.[23]

The practice of playing continuo parts in orchestral tuttis of piano concertos was standard in the late eighteenth century and continued well into the nineteenth. Mozart's most usual notation for the continuo in his concer-

tos was the term 'col basso', indicating that the keyboard player should play
from the string bass line. What appears to be a fully written-out continuo
part exists for the C major Concerto, K.246, although the purpose of the part
has been disputed.[24] Beethoven expected a continuo part to be played for all
of his piano concertos,[25] but although detailed notation for the part appears
in his scores, it has seldom been included in modern editions. By
Beethoven's time, however, the use of continuo in piano concertos was
beginning to die out: the score of Weber's Concerto, Op. 15 'contains
enough evidence to support the conclusion that its composer preferred the
soloist to be silent in all tuttis'.[26]

Texture and style

It is generally acknowledged in the early as well as the modern literature that a flamboyant style is less appropriate to the organ than to the
harpsichord.[27] It is also acknowledged that there were differences in the
national styles of Baroque continuo playing.[28] Recently, it has been argued
that changes in accompaniment styles took place over time.[29] Earlier writers,
too, commented on these changes. Heinichen wrote in 1728:

> It is well-known that in the old days shortly after its invention the
> thorough-bass was realised in only very few parts. Even during the
> last years of the previous century, it was not at all unusual to hear
> only a three-part realization . . . Later on, however, continuo
> playing in four parts became more fashionable, initially divided
> between both hands with two parts in the right and two parts in
> the left hand . . . (in this way one can still hear it practised today in
> certain contexts by eminent masters, particularly on the organ in
> soft music). This manner of realization, however, was not suitable
> in all contexts, particularly with the modern fast-moving basses . . .
> And so, the four-part accompaniment became divided unequally
> between the hands: three parts in the right hand and only the bass
> part in the left, the latter having the liberty to play the bass in
> octaves, provided that this was not rendered impossible by the
> tempo or too many fast notes.
> Today, this latter type of realization is the most common and the

Ex 7.1 Kirnberger's realisation of the continuo part from the trio sonata of Bach's *Musical Offering*, BWV 1079, third movement, bars 16–19

most fundamental; it is taught to all beginners . . . Those, however, who sufficiently master this art usually try to enrich the harmony even more – especially on harpsichords – and to play as full-voiced with the left hand as with the right. In this manner is then created a six-, seven- or eight-part realization, depending on the technical proficiency of the player. The more fully-voiced one accompanies with both hands, the more harmonious it sounds.[30]

The practice described by Heinichen, in which the bass part alone is played by the left hand while the right hand plays three-note chords, is widely described in sources of the second half of the seventeenth century and the first half of the eighteenth. The figured-bass teaching of Bach, Saint-Lambert and many others was based on this texture.[31] Written-out realisations such as the continuo part for the *Musical Offering* trio sonata by Bach's pupil Kirnberger (Ex. 7.1) largely follow this model. Not only was this sort of texture used by many in performance, but it was also important in the teaching of harmony. Its didactic purpose no doubt explains why many figured-bass teachers were so insistent that the rules governing consecutives and the proper preparation and resolution of dissonances should be observed.

Although strict four-part realisations are found in a number of early sources, it is also evident that keyboard players used a mixture of three- and four-part textures in their realisations at the keyboard. Arnold cites a number of examples[32] and in practice this kind of mixed texture is what many continuo players use today.

Four-part and mixed textures were popular in the second half of the seventeenth century and they continued to be used in the eighteenth century; but by this time a rather fuller kind of accompaniment was being used by many of the better harpsichordists in Europe. The full-voiced accompaniment described by Heinichen seems to have originated in Italy during the second half of the seventeenth century and then to have spread

Ex 7.2 Antonio Tonelli's realisation of Corelli's Sonata, Op. 5, No. 3, first movement, bars 10–13 (from Mortensen, "'Unerringly tasteful'?')

Ex 7.3 J. S. Bach, Sonata in B minor for flute, BWV 1030, slow movement, bars 9–11

into other parts of Europe. Italian examples survive (Ex. 7.2) and the style seems to be represented in written-out realisations by composers in other countries as, for example, in the slow movement of J. S. Bach's Sonata in B minor for flute and harpsichord where chords with five or more notes are consistently used (Ex. 7.3). That Bach was in the habit of producing full continuo parts is evident from Kittel's account:

> when Seb. Bach performed a piece of Church Music, one of his most capable pupils always had to accompany on the harpsichord

Ex 7.4 Gasparini, *L'armonico pratico*, Chapter 9

Ex 7.5 Chords with acciaccaturas, from an Italian MS (Williams, *Figured-bass accompaniment*, vol. I, p. 41)

> . . . One always had to be prepared often to find Bach's hands and fingers mingling with the hands and fingers of the player, and, without further troubling the latter, adorning the accompaniment with masses of harmony which were even more impressive than the unsuspected proximity of the stern preceptor.[33]

The texture of harpsichord realisations was enriched by the addition of ornaments as well as additional parts. Trills, appoggiaturas and mordents were encouraged in moderation, so long as they did not obscure the solo part.[34] Acciaccaturas were also encouraged between the notes of spread chords – their use is described in Italian, French and German sources (Ex. 7.4).[35] Italian practice also involved the simultaneous playing of acciaccaturas with other notes of a chord, followed by a rapid release of the non-harmony notes (Ex. 7.5). This sort of effect does not seem to have appealed to the French, who adopted a more restrained style than their Italian counterparts.[36]

Some keyboard sources for arias and sonatas survive with written-out right-hand parts that are similar in character to the obbligato lines played by solo instruments. It is unclear whether these keyboard sources represent the way in which keyboard performers frequently realised unfigured basses – Borgir argues for caution in interpreting at least some of them in this way.[37] However, early sources such as Heinichen, Saint-Lambert and C. P. E. Bach, describe a style in which the right hand imitates the soloist from time to time: 'opportunities will be found, especially in chamber and operatic arias without obbligato instruments, for imitation between soloist and the accompanist's right hand part'.[38] More than one account survives of J. S. Bach's playing in this style:

> Anyone who wants to have the right idea about what refinement in
> continuo-playing and very good accompaniment mean need only
> trouble himself to hear our Kapellmeister Bach here who plays
> every continuo to a solo in such a way that it might be thought an
> *obbligato* piece with the right-hand part composed previously.
> He could bring in imitations with his right hand or left hand so
> cleverly, or introduce a countersubject so unexpectedly, that listen-
> ers could not believe that it had not been very carefully pre-
> composed. He did not nevertheless neglect his duty of supporting
> the harmony . . . Generally speaking, his accompaniment through-
> out was as a solo part worked out with industrious care and of
> equal importance to the principal part – which was allowed to
> stand out at the right moments.[39]

In those arias or sonatas accompanied by continuo alone in which there are rests for the soloist it is often appropriate to play a keyboard ritornello, perhaps based on the opening phrase of the solo part, as often occurs in arias with instrumental accompaniment in the period. In passages of this sort the keyboard texture may be reduced to two parts. Other occasions on which thin textures are sometimes appropriate are where a fast-moving bass part is accompanied in thirds or tenths with the right hand – a technique described in a number of early sources.[40]

Fugal compositions require special treatment in the continuo part. It was normal practice in the Baroque for the keyboard continuo player to play in unison with the entries in a fugal texture, as Poglietti wrote '[at first] with one finger only, when the next voice enters, with two, and when the third voice enters, with three'.[41] Early continuo parts contain the fugal entries, not just in choral music, but in chamber music too. Some modern performers regard these written-in fugal entries as cues, but there seems no reason for regarding them in this way. Early continuo players appear to have played with the fugal entries in solo and trio sonatas, as the written-out parts for works such as Corelli's Op. 5 attest.

In some Baroque music all of the instrumental parts play in unison or in octaves for complete movements, or substantial passages, particularly in operatic or oratorio arias. In these instances specific directions are sometimes given to the continuo player by the Italian terms *tasto solo*, or *unisono*, which require that the keyboard player should play the bass line only, or in octaves with the bass. On those occasions where no such direction exists the keyboard player has to decide whether or not to play chords. Many nowadays accept as normal the performance of such passages without chords, but that view has been challenged.[42] While it is true that some bass lines lend themselves to chordal accompaniment better than others (a view expressed in C. P. E. Bach's tutor[43]), the presence of figures in unison textures probably suggest that chords should be played.

The advice of a great many early writers on figured-bass realisation is that the right hand of the continuo part should be kept low – well within the compass of the treble stave – so as not to create a 'vacuum' between the notes played by both hands. However, from Heinichen onwards some writers allow the harpsichordist to play higher. This is particularly appropriate in the full-voiced style, as examples 7.2 and 7.3 demonstrate.

The accompaniment of bass- or tenor-register instruments and voices poses a particular problem for the continuo player. If the keyboard part is in the same register as the soloist, too much doubling of the soloist's part may occur. Doubling of solo lines in any register was generally advised against in the early sources unless it was necessary to enable the soloist to find the notes. In the case of bass- or tenor-register solo parts, therefore, the options are to keep below the solo line (which is only achieved with difficulty, and perhaps not at all), or to play somewhat above it: the early sources differ in their advice.[44]

Finally, the continuo parts in Classical keyboard concertos raise their own particular problems. A variety of textures are needed: 'as a rule, the soloist plays continuo only when the double-basses are playing, and only if not excluded by rests entered in the left-hand staff of the keyboard part . . . The soloist plays non-stop in the middle register of the keyboard: mostly with both hands, occasionally with the left hand alone. First movements require a special approach: in long ritornellos, the soloist plays mostly with both hands . . . in short tuttis within solo blocks, the soloist plays mostly with the left hand alone or, rarely, not at all.'[45]

Plate XXVII

Fig. 7.1 Pasquali, *Thorough-bass made easy*, Plate XXVII

Recitative accompaniment

The performance of recitative allows keyboard players a great amount of freedom. Chords may be spread simply or elaborately, or all of the notes may be played simultaneously. The notes of chords may be sustained beneath the vocal part, or they may be released quickly. The performer's choices on these matters will depend on which instrument is used and the type of recitative being accompanied.

From the various eighteenth-century sources in which recitative accompaniment on the harpsichord is discussed it appears that chords were usually spread, but that the speed and extent of chord-spreading varied. C. P. E. Bach commented that 'the pace with which a chord is arpeggiated depends on the tempo and content of a recitative'.[46] His remarks are borne out by surviving realisations such as those in Pasquali's *Thorough-bass made easy* (Fig. 7.1), which show that the chords may be played from the bottom up, from the top down, or with a mixture of both. Other eighteenth-century examples include acciaccaturas between the notes of chords (see Ex. 7.4). However, there is not always time for arpeggiation (see Fig. 7.1), as C. P. E. Bach observed: 'arpeggiation must always be withheld from rapid declamation, especially when there are frequent chordal changes. For one thing, there is no time for it, and even if there were, it might very easily lead accompanist, singer, and audience into confusion.'[47]

The quick release of chords, so that the singer continues for short periods without any harmonic support, was practised in certain circumstances in the eighteenth century. Rogers, however, argues that this style was less usual in the eighteenth century than it has become in harpsichord-accompanied recitative today. In particular, Rogers criticises members of the 'Amsterdam school' (Leonhardt, Koopman and others) for what he considers to be an unwarranted over-emphasis on this style: 'even if the figuring prescribes a complete change of harmony over a bass pedal tone, frequently no chord is played . . . There is to my knowledge no evidence which would justify a blithe disregard of bass figuring in plain recitative.'[48] Nevertheless, Rogers concedes that there are places in the recitatives of Handel and others where short chords may be used, and he cites a number of recitatives where both short and sustained chords are used in close proximity.

Both long- and short-chord accompaniments were used on the organ in the eighteenth century. Heinichen, writing in 1711, indicates that both types of accompaniment were in use while later sources suggest that the short-chord style had become popular among German organists.[49] The practice of short-chord accompaniment enabled the singer to be heard distinctly and it appears that it is the most appropriate style of accompanying Bach's *secco* recitatives (*accompagnato* recitatives required sustained chords).

Controversy surrounds the way in which cadences are played in recitatives. Should the two chords of a cadence be played after the singer has finished, or should the first chord be played on the penultimate note in the voice part, with the final chord coming just after the singer has finished (the so-called 'foreshortened cadence')? Evidently in opera it was common for foreshortened cadences to be used in order to keep the action moving forwards, especially in lengthy recitatives with several cadences. Quantz wrote: 'in general the bass in all cadences of theatrical recitatives, whether accompanied with violins or plain, must begin its two notes, usually forming a descending leap of a fifth, during the last syllable; these notes must be performed in a lively manner, and must not be too slow'.[50] In many recitatives the bass notes are aligned with the voice part in the way suggested by Quantz, leading to comments such as those of Winton Dean: 'when Handel wrote a foreshortened cadence he meant it'.[51] Rogers has recently questioned whether the practice was as prevalent as it has been made out to be, but admits that many uncertainties remain in our knowledge of the performance practices of early recitatives.[52]

Notes

1 Stylistic awareness and keyboard music

1 See Colin Lawson and Robin Stowell, *The historical performance of music: an introduction* (Cambridge, 1999), Chapter 1 and Harry Haskell, *The early music revival* (London, 1988).

2 Louis Adam, *Méthode de Piano du Conservatoire* (Paris, 1804; R/1974), p. 233.

3 Carl Czerny, *Vollständige theoretisch-praktische Pianoforteschule Op. 500* (3 vols., Vienna, 1838–9); Eng. trans. as *Complete theoretical and practical pianoforte school, Op. 500* (London, 1838–9), Part 3, pp. 99–100.

4 Carl Czerny, *Supplement (oder vierter Theil) zur grossen Pianoforte Schule* (Vienna, 1846–7); Eng. trans. as *Supplement to Czerny's Royal pianoforte school* (London, 1846–7), pp. 107–8.

5 Robert Wangermée, 'Les premiers concerts historiques à Paris', *Mélanges Ernst Closson* (Brussels, 1948), pp. 185–96.

6 Review of the first of Moscheles' historical concerts in *The musical world* 4 (24 Feb. 1837), p. 156.

7 George Grove, ed., *A dictionary of music and musicians*, 1st edn (London, 1879), s.v. 'Harpsichord', by A. J. Hipkins.

8 François Joseph Fétis and Ignaz Moscheles, *Méthode des Méthodes de Piano* (Paris, 1840; R/1973), p. 73.

9 For a fuller discussion of the role of anthologies see Dorothy de Val and Cyril Ehrlich, 'Repertory and canon' in David Rowland, ed., *The Cambridge companion to the piano* (Cambridge, 1998), pp. 117–34.

10 Grove, ed., *A dictionary* 1 (1879), s.v. 'Harpsichord'.

11 Haskell, *The early music revival*, p. 45.

12 Further details can be found in Raymond Russell, *The harpsichord and clavichord*, 2nd edn by Howard Schott (London, 1973), pp. 122–3 and Donald Boalch, *Makers of the harpsichord and clavichord*, 3rd edn by Charles Mould (Oxford, 1995), pp. xix–xxxii.

13 William Dale, *Tschudi the harpsichord maker* (London, 1913), p. viii.

14 Raymond Russell, 'The harpsichord since 1800', *PRMA* 82 (1955/6), p. 64.

15 Ibid.

16 Edwin Ripin et al., *Early keyboard instruments* (London, 1989), p. 98.

17 The instruments are illustrated in John Henry van der Meer et al., *Kielklaviere* (Berlin, 1991). There is some doubt as to whether the Pleyel harpsichord now in Berlin is the instrument that was exhibited in 1889.

18 Ripin et al., *Early keyboard instruments*, pp. 99ff.

19 See Bernard Brauchli, *The clavichord* (Cambridge, 1998), Chapter 6.

20 Ibid., p. 278.

21 See Haskell, *The early music revival*, p. 190.

2 Repertory, performance and notation

1 See Dorothy de Val and Cyril Ehrlich, 'Repertory and Canon' in David Rowland, ed., *The Cambridge companion to the piano* (Cambridge, 1998), pp. 117–34.

2 Adolf Prosniz, *Handbuch der Clavierliteratur* (Vienna, 1887), Oscar Bie, *A history of the pianoforte and pianoforte players* (London, 1899; original German edn, 1898) and Max Seiffert, *Geschichte der Klaviermusik* (Leipzig, 1899).

3 See Robert Philip, 'Pianists on record in the twentieth century' in Rowland, ed., *The Cambridge companion to the piano*, pp. 75–95.

4 Some of the most comprehensive are Willi Apel and John Caldwell, eds., *Corpus of early keyboard music* (American Institute of Musicology, 1963–), Walter Georgii, ed., *Four hundred years of European keyboard music* (Cologne, 1959), Alexander Silbiger, ed., *17th century keyboard music: sources central to the keyboard art of the Baroque* (24 vols., New York, 1987–9) and Nicholas Temperley, ed., *The London piano school 1766–1860* (20 vols., New York and London, 1984–7).

5 Stanley Sadie, ed., *The New Grove dictionary of music and musicians* (London, 1980).

6 See, for example, John Harley, *British harpsichord music* (2 vols., Aldershot, 1992, 1994), vol. II, pp. 159, 167.

7 Grant O'Brien, *Ruckers: a harpsichord and virginal building tradition* (Cambridge, 1990), pp. 180–1 and 229.

8 See, for example, Rowland, *The Cambridge companion to the piano*, pp. 15ff., Richard Maunder, *Keyboard instruments in eighteenth-century Vienna* (Oxford, 1998), Chapter 7 and David Wainwright, *Broadwood by appointment* (London, 1982), pp. 101–2.

9 The issues are addressed in Colin Lawson and Robin Stowell, *The historical performance of music: an introduction* (Cambridge, 1999), especially Chapter 3.

10 Georg Muffat, *Florilegium secundum* (Passau, 1698), ed. Heinrich Rietsch (Graz, 1959).

11 Roland Jackson, *Performance practice, Medieval to contemporary* (New York, 1988) and Mary Vinquist and Neal Zaslaw, *Performance practice: a bibliography* (New York, 1971).

12 The issues are discussed in Lawson and Stowell, *The historical performance of music*, Chapter 2.

13 Carl Philipp Emanuel Bach, *Versuch über die wahre Art das Clavier zu spielen* (2 vols., Berlin, 1753, 1762), trans. and ed., William Mitchell (New York, 1949).

14 See Frederick Neumann, 'Facts and fiction about overdotting', *MQ* 63 (1977), pp. 155–85.

15 Lawson and Stowell, *The historical performance of music*, Chapter 2.

16 Ibid., John Caldwell, *Editing early music* (Oxford, 2/1995) and James Grier, *The critical editing of music* (Cambridge, 1996).

17 See, for example, the Associated Board, the *Neue Mozart Ausgabe* and Peters editions.

18 Temperley, ed., *The London pianoforte school 1766–1860*.

19 Ludwig van Beethoven, *The 32 piano sonatas* (London, Tecla Editions, 1980).

20 Chapters 2 and 3 of Carl Czerny, *Supplement (oder vierter Theil) zur grossen Pianoforte Schule* (Vienna, 1846–7), trans. as *Supplement to Czerny's Royal pianoforte school* (London, 1846–7), reprinted as *On the proper performance of all Beethoven's works for the piano*, ed. Paul Badura-Skoda (Vienna, 1970).

21 See the Introduction to Howard Ferguson's edition of Schubert's sonatas (London, The Associated Board, 1979).

22 Maunder, *Keyboard instruments, passim.*

3 The instruments

1 Clifford Bevan, *Musical instrument collections in the British Isles* (Winchester, 1990); the largest keyboard collections in the UK will be found in Fenton House (London), the Royal College of Music, the Finchcocks collection, the Victoria and Albert Museum, the Russell Collection (University of Edinburgh) and the Cobbe Collection (Hatchlands).

2 Donald Boalch, *Makers of the harpsichord and clavichord 1440–1840*, 3rd edn by Charles Mould (Oxford, 1995), pp. xix–xxxii.

3 Raymond Russell, *The harpsichord and clavichord*, 2nd edn by Howard Schott (London, 1973), Frank Hubbard, *Three centuries of harpsichord making* (Cambridge, Mass., 1965), Edwin Ripin et al., *Early keyboard instruments* (London, 1989 [the material is significantly updated from *The New Grove Dictionary* in which it first appeared]), and Grant O'Brien, *Ruckers; a harpsichord*

and virginal building tradition (Cambridge, 1990). Boalch, *Makers* is a dictionary of makers and list of surviving instruments.

4 See Christopher Page, 'In the direction of the beginning' in Howard Schott, ed., *The historical harpsichord* 1 (Stuyvesant, NY, 1984), p. 111, John Harley, *British harpsichord music* (2 vols., Aldershot, 1994), vol. II, pp. 150–1 and Elizabeth Wells, 'The London Clavicytherium', *EM* 6 (1978), pp. 568–71.

5 Edmund A. Bowles, 'A checklist of fifteenth-century representations of stringed keyboard instruments', in Edwin Ripin, ed., *Keyboard instruments: studies in organology* (Edinburgh, 1971; New York, 1977), pp. 11–18, Christopher Page and Lewis Jones, 'Four more 15th-century representations of stringed keyboard instruments', *GSJ* 31 (1978), pp. 151–4.

6 See O'Brien, *Ruckers* and John Koster, 'The importance of the early English harpsichord', *GSJ* 33 (1980), pp. 45–73.

7 John Barnes, 'The specious uniformity of Italian harpsichords' in Ripin, ed., *Keyboard instruments*, pp. 1–10, Denzil Wraight, 'Vicentius and the earliest harpsichords', *EM* 16 (1986), pp. 534–8, Denzil Wraight, 'The identification and authentication of Italian string keyboard instruments' in Howard Scott, ed., *The historical harpsichord* 3 (Stuyvesant, NY, 1992), pp. 59–161 and the relevant sections of Ripin et al., *Early keyboard instruments*.

8 See Christopher Stembridge, 'Music for the *cimbalo cromatico* and other split-keyed instruments in seventeenth-century Italy', *PPR* 5 (1992), pp. 5–41, Christopher Stembridge, 'The *cimbalo cromatico* and other Italian keyboard instruments with nineteen or more divisions to the octave', *PPR* 6 (1993), pp. 33–59 and Denzil Wraight and Christopher Stembridge, 'Italian split-keyed instruments with fewer than nineteen divisions to the octave', *PPR* 7 (1994), pp. 150–79.

9 See O'Brien, *Ruckers* and a useful summary by the same author in Ripin et al., *Early keyboard instruments*, pp. 29–44.

10 Many instruments of the eighteenth-century French school are documented by William Dowd, 'The surviving instruments of the Blanchet workshop' in Schott, ed., *The historical harpsichord* 1, pp. 17–107.

11 Boalch, *Makers*, entries for Fleischer.

12 Sheridan Germann, 'The Mietkes, the Margrave and Bach' in Peter Williams, ed., *Bach, Handel, Scarlatti: tercentenary essays* (Cambridge, 1985), p. 121.

13 Boalch, *Makers*, entries for Mietke.

14 See Richard Maunder, *Keyboard instruments in eighteenth-century Vienna* (Oxford, 1998).

15 See ibid., passim.

16 See Koster, 'The importance of the early English harpsichord'.

17 Ibid.

18 See, for example, Ripin et al., *Early keyboard instruments*, pp. 95–6 and Russell, *The harpsichord and clavichord*, Chapter 8.

19 Thomas Mace, *Musick's monument* (London, 1676; R/1958), pp. 235–6.

20 Boalch, *Makers*, pp. 176–7 and Edwin Ripin, 'Expressive devices applied to the eighteenth-century harpsichord', *Organ Yearbook* 1 (1970), pp. 64–80.

21 See John Koster, 'Foreign influences in eighteenth-century French piano making', *EKJ* 11 (1993), pp. 9–10 and Ripin, 'Expressive devices'.

22 See Boalch, *Makers*, Michael Cole, *The pianoforte in the Classical era* (Oxford, 1997), p. 116 and Ripin, 'Expressive devices'.

23 Ripin et al., *Early keyboard instruments*, p. 131.

24 O'Brien, *Ruckers*, Chapter 3.

25 Boalch, *Makers*, p. 714.

26 Bernard Brauchli, *The clavichord* (Cambridge, 1998). See also Francis Knights, 'The clavichord: a comprehensive bibliography', *GSJ* 48 (1995), pp. 53–67.

27 See the preface to *Ars magna consoni et dissoni*, by Johann Speth (Augsburg), quoted in Brauchli, *Clavichord*, p. 101.

28 Rosamond Harding, *The piano-forte* (Old Woking, 2/1978), Cyril Ehrlich, *The piano* (Oxford, 2/1990).

29 Stewart Pollens, *The early pianoforte* (Cambridge, 1995), Cole, *The pianoforte* and Maunder, *Keyboard instruments*.

30 Dominic Gill, *The book of the piano* (Oxford, 1981), David Rowland, ed., *The Cambridge companion to the piano* (Cambridge, 1998), Edwin Ripin et al., *The Piano* (London, 1988).

31 Pollens, *The early pianoforte*, Chapter 3.

32 Maffei's text is translated in Pollens, *The early pianoforte*, pp. 57–61 and partially translated in Harding, *The piano-forte*, pp. 5–6.

33 Ferrini's pianos are described in Pollens, *The early pianoforte*, Chapter 4.

34 Details of Scarlatti's association with the piano will be found in Rowland, ed., *The Cambridge companion to the piano*, pp. 8–9 and Pollens, *The early pianoforte*, pp. 118–19.

35 Pollens, *The early pianoforte*, Chapter 5.

36 Rowland, ed., *The Cambridge companion to the piano*, pp. 15–16.

37 Cole, *The pianoforte*, p. 22.

38 The action is described in Lorenz Mizler, *Neu eröffnete musikalische Bibliothek*, vol. III, part 3 (Leipzig, 1747), pp. 474–7.

39 See Rowland, ed., *The Cambridge companion to the piano*, pp. 11–12 and Eva Badura-Skoda, 'Aspects of performance practice', in Robert L. Marshall, ed., *Eighteenth-century keyboard music* (New York, 1994), p. 59. For details of Silbermann's pianos see Pollens, *The early pianoforte*, Chapter 6.

40 Koster, 'Foreign influences', pp. 7–12.

41 Details of J. H. Silbermann's pianos can be found in Harding, *The piano-forte*, p. 38, Pollens, *The early pianoforte*, p. 221 and Koster, 'Foreign influences', pp. 12–17.

42 See John Koster, 'Foreign influences', pp. 17–18 and 'Two early French grand pianos', *EKJ* 12 (1994), pp. 7–37.

43 See Pollens, *The early pianoforte*, pp. 186ff.

44 See Cole, *The pianoforte*, Chapter 9.

45 A full discussion of the history of the keyed pantalon can be found in ibid., Chapter 2.

46 See ibid., pp. 195–6.

47 Described in detail in Pollens, *The early pianoforte*, pp. 98–107.

48 Cole, *The pianoforte*, pp. 45–6, 129, 183 and Chapter 14.

49 For a detailed study of Backers' work and the subsequent history of the English grand piano see ibid., Chapters 7 and 8.

50 See ibid. for details.

51 See David Rowland, 'Piano music and keyboard compass in the 1790s', *EM* 27 (1999), pp. 283–93.

52 Richard Maunder, 'The earliest English square piano', *GSJ* 42 (1989), pp. 77–84. See Cole, *The pianoforte* for the most detailed description of the development of the English square.

53 J. Gallay, *Un inventaire sous la terreur. Etat des instruments de musique relevés chez les émigrés et condamnés par H. Bruni* (Paris, 1890).

54 John Koster, 'Two early French grand pianos', pp. 7–37.

55 See Cole, *The pianoforte*, Chapter 11 and Maunder, *Keyboard instruments*, Chapter 5.

56 See Maunder, *Keyboard instruments*, pp. 114–15 and Rowland, 'Piano music and keyboard compass'.

57 Stanley Sadie, ed., *The New Grove dictionary of music and musicians* (London, 1980), s.v. 'Temperaments' provides a useful introduction to the subject. Charles Padgham's *The well-tempered organ* (Oxford, 1986) is used by many tuners for its detailed information on a wide variety of temperaments. Another comprehensive volume is Owen Jorgensen's *Tuning the historical temperaments by ear* (Marquette, Mich., 1977). Useful, brief summaries are Martin B. Tittle, *A performer's guide through historical keyboard tunings* (Ann Arbor, Mich., 1978) and Gerrit Klop, *Harpsichord tuning* (Garderen, 1974).

58 See Vincent J. Panetta, trans. and ed., *Treatise on harpsichord tuning by Jean Denis* (Cambridge, 1987), pp. 37ff. Ruckers harpsichords had additional strings to cope with the problems of meantone tunings – see O'Brien, *Ruckers*, pp. 220–1.

59 A useful and relatively brief discussion will be found in Mark Lindley, 'J. S. Bach's tunings', *MT* 126 (1985), pp. 721–6.

60 Ibid.

61 Owen H. Jorgensen, *Tuning: containing the perfection of eighteenth-century temperament, the lost art of nineteenth-century temperament, and the science of equal temperament* (East Lansing, Mich., 1991).

62 Significant exhibitions are held in a variety of cities, including York, Bruges, Boston, Berkeley and others.

63 The number of cents by which a note deviates from equal temperament can be found in sources such as Padgham, *The well-tempered organ* and can be measured by many of the cheaper meters.

4 Use of instruments and technique

1 Further discussions of terminology can be found in a number of sources, including John Harley, *British harpsichord music* (2 vols., Aldershot, 1994), vol. II, pp. 149–57, Edwin Ripin *et al.*, *Early keyboard instruments* (London, 1989), Appendix 1, Richard Maunder, *Keyboard instruments in eighteenth-century Vienna* (Oxford, 1998), Chapter 2, and Bruce Gustafson and David Fuller, *A catalogue of French harpsichord music 1699–1780* (Oxford, 1990), preface.

2 Praetorius, *Syntagma musicum* (Wolfenbüttel, 1614–15; R/1959), p. 62.

3 See Harley, *British harpsichord music*, vol. II, pp. 150ff. for a fuller discussion.

4 Ibid., vol. II, p. 155.

5 Grant O'Brien, *Ruckers: a harpsichord and virginal building tradition* (Cambridge, 1990), p. xix.

6 Harley, *British harpsichord music*, vol. II, p. 152 note 14.

7 Maunder, *Keyboard instruments*, pp. 6–11.

8 See ibid., pp. 6, 11–12. Eva Badura-Skoda, 'Prolegomena to a history of the Viennese fortepiano', *Israel studies in musicology* 2 (1980), p. 87, takes a different view.

9 Information from London newspapers kindly made available to me by Richard Maunder. See also Leon Plantinga, *Clementi: his life and music* (Oxford, 1979), pp. 35–9.

10 Richard Maunder, 'Mozart's keyboard instruments', *EM* 23 (1992), pp. 207–19.

11 See Peter Williams, *The organ music of J. S. Bach*, vol. III, *A background* (Cambridge, 1984), pp. 47ff.

12 Bernard Brauchli, *The clavichord* (Cambridge, 1998), p. 155.

13 Bruce Gustafson, *French harpsichord music of the 17th century* (3 vols., Ann Arbor, Mich., 1979), vol. I, pp. 1–2.

14 See, for example, Harley, *British harpsichord music*, vol. II, esp. pp. 162–4, O'Brien, *Ruckers*, pp. 226–7, Ripin et al., *Early keyboard instruments*, pp. 12, 27–8, 42, 62 and Appendix 1.

15 See Kenneth Gilbert, 'Le clavecin français et la registration' in Edith Weber, ed., *L'interprétation de la musique française aux XVIIe et XVIIIe siècles* (Paris, 1974), pp. 203–11, David Fuller, ed., *A. L. Couperin: selected works for keyboard*, vol. I (Madison, Wisc., 1975), preface, and David Fuller, 'Harpsichord registration', *Diapason* 69 (July 1978), pp. 1, 6–7.

16 O'Brien, *Ruckers*, p. 226.

17 John Koster, 'The importance of the early English harpsichord', *GSJ* 33 (1980), p. 69.

18 Donald Boalch, *Makers of the harpsichord and clavichord*, 3rd edn by Charles Mould (Oxford, 1995), p. 84.

19 Thomas Mace, *Musick's monument* (London, 1676; R/1958), p. 235.

20 Harley, *British harpsichord music*, vol. I, p. 68.

21 Ibid., vol. II, p. 164.

22 Quirinus van Blankenburg, *Elementa musica* (The Hague, 1739), p. 145, translated in Edwin Ripin, 'Expressive devices applied to the eighteenth-century harpsichord', *Organ yearbook* 1 (1970), p. 65.

23 A facsimile is published in Garland's complete edition of C. P. E. Bach's works (New York and London, 1985).

24 See Gilbert, 'Le clavecin français', p. 204.

25 A list of publications and registration directions is in ibid., p. 207.

26 Bruce Gustafson, ed., *Four symphonies concertantes for harpsichord and piano with orchestra ad libitum* (Madison, Wisc., 1995).

27 Fuller, ed., *A. L. Couperin: selected works for keyboard*.

28 See in particular Michael Cole, *The pianoforte in the Classical era* (Oxford, 1997), Stewart Pollens, *The early pianoforte* (Cambridge, 1995), Sandra Rosenblum, *Performance practices in Classic piano music* (Bloomington, 1988), David Rowland, *A history of pianoforte pedalling* (Cambridge, 1993) and David Rowland, 'Beethoven's pianoforte pedalling' in Robin Stowell, ed., *Performing Beethoven* (Cambridge, 1994).

29 Pollens, *The early pianoforte*, pp. 73, 151–2.

30 Ibid., pp. 181–2.

31 See Cole, *The pianoforte*, p. 75.

32 C. P. E . Bach, *Versuch über die wahre Art das Clavier zu spielen* (2 vols., Berlin, 1753, 1762), trans. and ed. William Mitchell (London, 1974), p. 431.

33 Charles Burney, *Music, men and manners in France and Italy*, ed. H. E. Poole (London, 2/1974), pp. 19–20.

34 Johann Peter Milchmeyer, *Die wahre Art das Pianoforte zu spielen* (Dresden, 1797), Chapter 5 (trans. in Rowland, *A history of pianoforte pedalling*, pp. 159–69).

35 Rowland, *A history of pianoforte pedalling*, Chapter 3.

36 Charles Chaulieu, 'Des pédales du piano', *Le pianiste* 9 (Paris, 1833–4), p. 132.

37 Useful summaries of early comments on technique will be found in Brauchli, *Clavichord*, Chapter 7, Reginald Gerig, *Famous pianists and their technique* (Washington and New York, 1974), Chapter 2 and Rosenblum, *Performance practices*, Chapter 6.

38 C. P. E. Bach, *Versuch*, trans., pp. 42–3.

39 Johann Nikolaus Forkel, *Über Johann Sebastian Bach's Leben* (Leipzig, 1802), trans. by A. C. F. Kollman in 1820 and reprinted in Hans T. David and Arthur Mendel, *The Bach reader* (New York and London, 1972), p. 308.

40 Charles Burney, *An account of the musical performances* (London, 1785; R/1964), 'Sketch of the life of Handel', p. 35.

41 David and Mendel, *The Bach reader*, pp. 307–8.

42 Jean-Philippe Rameau, preface to *Pièces de clavecin* (Paris, 1724), trans. Erwin R. Jacobi (Kassel, 1972), p. 17.

43 Emily Anderson, trans. and ed., *The letters of Mozart and his family* (London, 1985), p. 339.

44 Eliot Forbes, ed., *Thayer's life of Beethoven* (Princeton, 1967), p. 337.

45 Mark Lindley and Maria Boxall, *Early keyboard fingerings: a comprehensive guide* (London, 1992).

46 Useful overviews of aspects of the subject will be found in Howard Ferguson, *Keyboard interpretation from the 14th to the 19th century: an introduction* (London, 2/1987), Chapter 5, Mark Lindley, 'Keyboard fingerings and articulation' in Howard Mayer Brown and Stanley Sadie, eds., *Performance practice: music after 1600* (London, 1989), pp. 186–203 and Rosenblum, *Performance practices*, pp. 190–215.

47 Peter le Huray, 'English keyboard fingerings in the 16th and early 17th centuries' in Ian Bent, ed., *Source materials and the interpretation of music: a memorial volume to Thurston Dart* (London, 1981), pp. 227–57, Desmond Hunter, 'The implications of fingering indications in virginalist sources: some thoughts for further study', *PPR* 5 (1992), pp. 123–38 and John Morehen, 'Aiding authentic performance: a fingering databank for Elizabethan keyboard music', *Computing in musicology: an international directory of applications* 9 (1993–4), pp. 81–92.

48 For a brief discussion in English see John Butt, 'Germany and the Netherlands' in Alexander Silbiger, ed., *Keyboard music before 1700* (New York, 1995), pp. 172–5.

49 Mark Lindley, 'Keyboard technique and articulation: evidence for the performance practices of Bach, Handel and Scarlatti' in Peter Williams, ed., *Bach, Handel, Scarlatti: tercentenary essays* (Cambridge, 1985), pp. 207–43.

50 See Haydn's sonata Hob.XVI:42, first movement, bar 23 and 45, third movement, bar 20 and Mozart's finger studies published in the *Neue Mozart Ausgabe, Klavierstücke* II, p. 172.

51 See especially Rosenblum, *Performance practices*, pp. 209–15 and William Newman, *Beethoven on Beethoven: playing his music his way* (New York and London, 1988), pp. 284–300.

52 Patrick Piggott, *The life and music of John Field 1782–1837* (London, 1973), pp. 106–9, Jean-Jacques Eigeldinger, *Chopin vu par ses élèves* (Neuchâtel, 1970), trans. Naomi Shohet, ed. Roy Howat as *Chopin: pianist and teacher* (Cambridge, 1986), pp. 244–66.

53 C. P. E. Bach, *Versuch*, trans., p. 42.

54 Daniel Gottlob Türk, *Klavierschule* (Leipzig and Halle, 1789), trans. Raymond H. Haggh (Lincoln, Nebr., 1982), pp. 131–41.

55 See the discussion of articulation in Chapter 3 of Colin Lawson and Robin Stowell, *The historical performance of music* (Cambridge, 1999).

56 Friedrich Wilhelm Marpurg, *Anleitung zum Clavierspielen* (Berlin, 1755, 2/1765; R (1765 edn)/1970), p. 29; trans. Bernard Harrison, *Haydn's keyboard music* (Oxford, 1997), p. 41.

57 Further discussions of the subject will be found in Rosenblum, *Performance practices*, Chapter 5 and Harrison, *Haydn's keyboard music,* Chapter 2.

58 Muzio Clementi, *Introduction to the art of playing on the pianoforte* (London, 1801; R/1974), p. 9.

59 Carl Czerny, 'Recollections from my life', trans. Ernest Saunders, *MQ* 42 (1956), p. 307.

60 See Brauchli, *Clavichord*, pp. 270–1.

61 Türk, *Klavierschule*, trans., p. 281.

62 C. P. E. Bach, *Versuch*, trans., p. 126.

63 Brauchli, *Clavichord*, p. 274.

5 Non-notated and notated issues

1 Peter Williams, *The organ music of J. S. Bach* (3 vols., Cambridge, 1984), vol. III, pp. 43–7.

2 *Spenersche Zeitung* (11 May 1747), trans. Christoph Wolff, 'New research on Bach's *Musical Offering'*, *MQ* 57 (1971), p. 401.

3 See Katalin Komlós, *Fortepianos and their music* (Oxford, 1995), p. 144.

4 C. P. E. Bach, *Versuch über die wahre Art das Clavier zu spielen* (2 vols., Berlin, 1753, 1762), Chapter 7.

5 Otto Erich Deutsch, *Mozart. A Documentary biography* (London, 2/1966), p. 543.

6 See Komlós, *Fortepianos*, pp. 144–5.

7 Continuo solos and *partimenti* are discussed in Tharald Borgir, *The performance of the basso continuo in Italian Baroque music* (Ann Arbor, Mich., 1987), esp. Chapter 19.

8 Willi Apel and John Caldwell, eds., *Corpus of early keyboard music*, vol. VII (American Institute of Musicology, 1968).

9 François Couperin, *L'Art de toucher le Clavecin* (Paris, 1717), trans. and ed. Mevanwy Roberts (Leipzig, 1933), p. 33.

10 C. P. E. Bach, *Versuch*, trans. William J. Mitchell (London, 1949; R/1974), p. 431.

11 Nicholas Temperley, ed., *The London Piano School 1766–1860* (20 vols., New York and London, 1984), vol. II.

12 David Rowland, ed., *The Cambridge companion to the piano* (Cambridge, 1998), p. 64.

13 Girolamo Frescobaldi, *Toccate d'intavolatura di cembalo et organo . . . libro primo* (1637), preface, trans. and ed. Pierre Pidoux (Kassel, 1967).

14 Useful discussions of the subject will be found in Colin Lawson and Robin Stowell, *The historical performance of music: an introduction* (Cambridge, 1999) and Frederick Neumann, *Performance practices of the seventeenth and eighteenth centuries* (New York, 1993).

15 Frederick Neumann, *The ornamentation of Baroque and post-Baroque music* (Princeton, 1983), pp. 546–7.

16 Existing cadenzas of the period are discussed in Philip Whitmore, *Unpremeditated art: the cadenza in the classical keyboard concerto* (Oxford, 1991).

17 C. P. E. Bach, *Versuch*, trans., p. 143.

18 Brief cadenzas are required in Haydn's sonatas Hob.XVI:6/iii, 19/ii and 46/ii, according to Bernard Harrison, *Haydn's keyboard music* (Oxford, 1997), p. 163, and there are several examples among the sonatas of J. C. Bach's Op. 5.

19 Daniel Gottlob Türk, *Klavierschule* (Leipzig and Halle, 1789), trans. Raymond H. Haggh (Lincoln, Nebr., 1982), p. 290.

20 These and others of Mozart's cadenzas are discussed in detail in Whitmore, *Unpremeditated art*, Chapter 8.

21 Türk, *Klavierschule*, trans., pp. 297–309.

22 Johann Joachim Quantz, *Versuch einer Anweisung, die Flöte traversiere zu spielen* (Berlin, 1752, 3/1789; R/1952), trans. Edward R. Reilly (London, 2/1985), p. 335.

23 François Couperin, *Pièces de clavecin: troisième livre* (Paris, 1722), preface, trans. in Lawson and Stowell, *The historical performance of music*, p. 68.

24 See, for example, the preface to C. P. E. Bach's *Sonaten für Clavier mit veränderten Reprisen* (keyboard sonatas with varied reprises) of 1760 and Türk's *Klavierschule*, trans., p. 310.

25 Türk, *Klavierschule*, trans., p. 311.

26 C. P. E. Bach, *The collected works for solo keyboard*, vol. II (New York and London, 1985).

27 Harrison, *Haydn's keyboard music*, Chapter 4.

28 Charles Rosen, *The Classical style* (London, 1971), p. 101.

29 Johann Peter Milchmeyer, *Die wahre Art das Pianoforte zu spielen* (Dresden, 1797); trans. in Komlós, *Fortepianos*, p. 124.

30 See, for example, Harrison, *Haydn's keyboard music*, pp. 155ff. and Robert D. Levin, 'Improvised embellishments in Mozart's keyboard music', *EM* 20 (1992), pp. 221–33.

31 Levin, 'Improvised embellishments', p. 226.

32 Emily Anderson, trans. and ed., *The letters of Beethoven* (London, 1961), letter of 12 Feb. 1816.

33 Johann Nepomuk Hummel, *Ausführliche theoretisch-practische Anweisung zum Pianoforte-Spiele* (Vienna, 1828), trans. as *A complete theoretical and practical course of instruction on the art of playing the pianoforte* (London, 1828), Part 1, p. 66.

34 Richard Hudson, *Stolen time: the history of Tempo Rubato* (Oxford, 1994).

35 A useful summary will be found in Neumann, *Performance practices*, pp. 36ff.

36 See note 9 above.

37 Jean-Philippe Rameau, *Observations sur notre instinct pour la musique* (Paris, 1754), p. vii and Jean-Jacques Rousseau, *Dictionnaire de musique* (Paris, 1768; R/1969), s.v. 'Mouvement'.

38 See, for example, Türk's *Klavierschule*, trans., pp. 363–4.

39 C. P. E. Bach, *Versuch*, trans., pp. 160–1.

40 Sandra Rosenblum, *Performance practices in Classic piano music* (Bloomington, 1991), Chapter 10.

41 Türk, *Klavierschule*, trans., p. 360.

42 Leopold Mozart, *Versuch einer gründlichen Violinschule* (Augsburg, 1756), trans. Editha Knocker as *A Treatise on the fundamental principles of violin playing* (London, 1951), pp. 223–4.

43 Emily Anderson, trans. and ed., *The letters of Mozart and his family* (London, 3/1985), pp. 339–40.

44 Hummel, *A complete theoretical and practical course*, Part 3, p. 53.

45 Franz Gerhard Wegeler and Ferdinand Ries, *Biographische Notizen über Beethoven* (Koblenz, 1838; R/1972), trans. in William Newman, *Beethoven on Beethoven* (New York and London, 1988), p. 112.

46 See Jean-Jacques Eigeldinger, *Chopin vu par ses élèves*, trans. Naomi Shohet, ed. Roy Howat as *Chopin: pianist and teacher* (Cambridge, 1986), p. 267.

47 Friedrich Wieck, *Clavier und Gesang* (Leipzig, 1853), trans. and ed. Henry Pleasants as *Piano and song* (New York, 1988), p. 140.

48 See, for example, David Rowland, 'Chopin's tempo rubato in context' in John Rink and Jim Samson, eds., *Chopin Studies 2* (Cambridge, 1994), pp. 206–8.

49 Couperin, *L'Art de toucher*, trans., p. 15.

50 Pierre-Claude Foucquet, *Pièces de Clavecin, Livre II* (Paris 1751), preface, trans. in Hudson, *Stolen time*, p. 25.

51 Antoine Forqueray, *Pièces de clavecin*, ed. Colin Tilney (Paris, 1970), p. 74.

52 See Hudson, *Stolen time*, Chapter 5.

53 Anderson, ed., *The letters of Mozart*, p. 340.

54 See especially Hudson, *Stolen time* and Rowland, 'Chopin's rubato'.

55 Carl Mikuli, *Vorwort* to his edition of Chopin's works (Leipzig, 1880), trans. in Eigeldinger, *Chopin: pianist and teacher*, p. 49.

56 John Butt, *Bach interpretation: articulation marks in primary sources of J. S. Bach* (Cambridge, 1990), p. 208.

57 Trans. by Rebecca Harris-Warrick as *Principles of the harpsichord* (Cambridge, 1984).

58 Ibid., p. 29.

59 Ibid., p. 31.

60 Ibid., p. 86.

61 C. P. E. Bach, *Versuch*, trans., p. 155.

62 Louis Adam, *Méthode de piano du Conservatoire* (Paris, 1804), p. 151.

63 David Rowland, *A history of pianoforte pedalling* (Cambridge, 1993), p. 50.

64 Lawson and Stowell, *The historical performance of music*, Chapter 3.

65 C. P. E. Bach, *Versuch*, trans., p. 150.

66 Carl Czerny, *Vollständige theoretisch-praktische Pianoforteschule, Op.500* (3 vols., Vienna, 1838–9), trans. as *Complete theoretical and practical pianoforte school, Op.500* (London, 1838–9), vol. III, pp. 55–6. See also Harrison, *Haydn's keyboard music*, Chapter 9 and Rosenblum, *Performance practices*, pp. 285ff. for further discussions.

67 Türk, *Klavierschule*, trans., p. 282.

68 Milchmeyer, *Die wahre Art das Pianoforte zu spielen*, p. 38.

6 Case studies

1 Bruce Gustafson, 'France' in Alexander Silbiger, ed., *Keyboard music before 1700* (New York, 1995), p. 126.

2 Davitt Moroney, ed., *Pièces de clavecin de Louis Couperin* (Monaco, 1985), Introduction, p. 10.

3 Ibid.

4 See, for example, David Ledbetter, 'What the lute sources tell us about the performances of French harpsichord music' in Peter Dirksen, ed., *The harpsichord
and its repertoire* (Utrecht, 1992) and Silbiger, ed., *Keyboard music before 1700*,
pp. 121ff.

5 See Richard Troeger, 'The French unmeasured harpsichord prelude: notation
and performance', *EKJ* 10 (1992), pp. 89–119 and Davitt Moroney, 'The performance of unmeasured harpsichord preludes', *EM* 4 (1976), pp. 143–51.

6 Colin Tilney, *The art of the unmeasured prelude* (London, 1991).

7 Troeger, 'The French unmeasured harpsichord prelude', p. 101.

8 The precise function and meaning of the slurs of Couperin's preludes is discussed
at length in the introduction to Moroney's edition.

9 Facsimile, with introduction by David Kinsela (Gregg International, Godstone,
Surrey, 1985).

10 For a recent discussion see John Koster, 'The quest for Bach's *Clavier*: an his-
toriographical interpretation', *EKJ* 14 (1996), pp. 65–84.

11 Raymond Russell, *The harpsichord and clavichord*, 2nd edn by Howard Schott
(London, 1971), pp. 107–8 and Frank Hubbard, *Three centuries of harpsichord
making* (Cambridge, Mass., 1965), pp. 184, 331–3.

12 See especially Sheridan Germann, 'The Mietkes, the Margrave and Bach' in Peter
Williams, ed., *Bach, Handel, Scarlatti: tercentenary essays* (Cambridge, 1985), pp.
119–48.

13 Ibid., pp. 133–4 gives a full description of the characteristics of Mietke's instruments.

14 Donald H. Boalch, *Makers of the harpsichord and clavichord*, 3rd edn by Charles
Mould (Oxford, 1995), s.v. 'Mietke'.

15 For some recent comments on the issue see Matthew Dirst, 'Bach's French over-
tures and the politics of overdotting', *EM* 25 (1997), pp. 35–44 and Ido Abravaya,
'A French overture revisited', *EM* 25 (1997), pp. 47–61.

16 See Michael Collins, 'A reconsideration of French over-dotting', *ML* 1 (1969),
pp. 111–23.

17 See Frederick Neumann, 'The question of rhythm in the two versions of Bach's
French Overture, BWV 831' in Robert Marshall, ed., *Studies in Renaissance and
Baroque music in honor of Arthur Mendel* (Kassel, 1974), pp. 183–94.

18 A brief description will be found in Colin Lawson and Robin Stowell, *The historical performance of music: an introduction* (Cambridge, 1999), Chapter 3. A more
extensive study is Stephen Hefling's *Rhythmic alteration in seventeenth- and
eighteenth-century music* (New York, 1993).

19 Frederick Neumann, *Performance practices of the seventeenth and eighteenth centuries* (New York, 1993), p. 133.

20 Hefling, *Rhythmic alteration*, p. 61.

21 See Silbiger, ed., *Keyboard music before 1700*, p. 18.

22 Silbiger, ed., *Keyboard music before 1700*, p. 127.

23 See Hugh MacDonald, 'To repeat or not to repeat?', *PRMA* 111 (1984–5), pp. 121–38.

24 See Bernard Harrison, *Haydn's keyboard music* (Oxford, 1997) and Richard Maunder, *Keyboard instruments in eighteenth-century Vienna* (Oxford, 1998).

25 Horst Walter, 'Haydns Klaviere', *Haydn-Studien* 2 (1970), p. 258.

26 See Maunder, *Keyboard instruments*, p. 100.

27 Maunder, *Keyboard instruments*, esp. pp. 97–100.

28 See, for example, Clive Brown, 'Dots and strokes in late 18th- and 19th-century music', *EM* 21 (1993), pp. 593–610 and Frederick Neumann, 'Dots and strokes in Mozart', *EM* 21 (1993), pp. 429–35.

29 Harrison, *Haydn's keyboard music*, Chapter 2.

30 Emily Anderson, trans. and ed., *The letters of Mozart and his family* (London, 3/1985).

31 Michael Cole, *The pianoforte in the Classical era* (Oxford, 1998), pp. 208–11.

32 Anderson, ed., *The letters of Mozart*.

33 Richard Maunder & David Rowland, 'Mozart's pedal piano', *EM* 23 (1995), pp. 287–96.

34 Otto Erich Deutsch, *Mozart: a documentary biography* (London, 2/1966), p. 239.

35 Eva and Paul Badura-Skoda, *Interpreting Mozart on the keyboard* (London, 1962; R/1986), Chapter 8.

36 See H. C. Robbins Landon, ed., *The Mozart compendium* (London, 1990), p. 267.

37 Maunder, *Keyboard instruments*, p. 112.

38 William Newman, *Beethoven on Beethoven* (New York and London, 1988), Chapter 3.

39 Emily Anderson, trans. and ed., *The letters of Beethoven* (London, 1961).

40 See David Rowland, 'Beethoven's pianoforte pedalling' in Robin Stowell, ed., *Performing Beethoven* (Cambridge, 1994), pp. 51–2.

41 This issue and others relating to compass is explored in further detail in Maunder, *Keyboard instruments*, pp. 114–15 and in David Rowland, 'Piano music and keyboard compass in the 1790s', *EM* 27 (1999), pp. 283–93.

42 For a general discussion of Beethoven's pedalling see Rowland, 'Beethoven's pianoforte pedalling', pp. 49–69.

43 Carl Czerny, *Supplement (oder vierter Theil) zur grossen Pianoforte Schule* (Vienna, 1846–7), trans. as *Supplement to Czerny's Royal pianoforte school* (London, 1846–7), p. 2.

44 Czerny, *Supplement*, trans., p. 107.

45 In Gustav Nottebohm, *Zweite Beethoveniana* (Leipzig, 1887), trans. in Newman, *Beethoven on Beethoven*, p. 239.
46 Jim Samson, *Chopin* (Oxford, 1996), pp. 270–81.
47 Ibid., p. 280.
48 A number of remarks relevant to the subject will be found in Jean-Jacques Eigeldinger, *Chopin vu par ses élèves*, trans. Naomi Shohet, ed. Roy Howat as *Chopin: pianist and teacher* (Cambridge, 1986), pp. 52ff.
49 Jan Ekier's Wiener Urtext Edition of the nocturnes (1980), p. XIV.
50 Quoted and translated in Eigeldinger, *Chopin: pianist and teacher*, p. 77.
51 Quoted and translated in ibid., p. 49.
52 Quoted and translated in ibid., p. 77.
53 Quoted and translated in ibid., p. 49.
54 Jean Kleczynski, *How to play Chopin*, trans. Alfred Whittingham (London, 1913), p. 49.
55 Quoted and translated in Eigeldinger, *Chopin: pianist and teacher*, p. 52.

7 Continuo realisation

1 Frank T. Arnold, *The art of accompaniment from a thorough-bass* (London, 1931; R/1961), Peter Williams, *Figured bass accompaniment* (2 vols., Edinburgh, 1970).
2 Tharald Borgir, *The performance of the basso continuo in Italian Baroque music* (Ann Arbor, Mich., 1987), George J. Buelow, *Thorough-bass accompaniment according to Johann David Heinichen* (Ann Arbor, Mich., 1986), Laurence Dreyfus, *Bach's continuo group* (Cambridge, Mass., 1987), Patrick J. Rogers, *Continuo realization in Handel's vocal music* (Ann Arbor, Mich., 1989).
3 The best available sources in translation are C. P. E. Bach, *Versuch über die wahre Art das Clavier zu spielen* (2 vols., Berlin, 1753, 1762), trans. and ed. W. Mitchell (New York, 1949; R/1974), Francesco Gasparini, *L'armonico pratico al cimbalo* (Venice, 1708), trans. F. Stillings (New Haven, Conn., 1963) and Johann Joachim Quantz, *Versuch einer Anweisung, die Flöte traversiere zu spielen* (Berlin, 1752, 3/1789; R/1958), trans. Edward R. Reilly (London, 2/1985). See also David Ledbetter, ed., *Continuo playing according to Handel* (Oxford, 1990) and Pamela Poulin, ed., *J. S. Bach's precepts and principles for playing the thorough-bass or accompanying in four parts* (Oxford, 1994).
4 Arnold, *The art of accompaniment*, pp. 803ff. and Williams, *Figured bass accompaniment*, vol. II, p. 3.
5 See also Buelow, *Thorough-bass accompaniment*, Chapter 3.
6 C. P. E. Bach, *Versuch*, trans., p. 173.

7   This information and much of what follows in this paragraph is based on the
    observations in Borgir, *The performance of the basso continuo*.

8   A lively debate took place in vol. 24 (1996) of *EM*: see Peter Walls, 'Performing
    Corelli's violin sonatas, Op. 5', pp. 133–42, John Holloway, 'Corelli's Op. 5: text,
    act . . . and reaction', pp. 635–40, David Watkin, 'Corelli's Op. 5 sonatas: "Violino
    e violone *o* cimbalo"', pp. 645–63 and Lars Ulrik Mortensen, '"Unerringly taste-
    ful"?: harpsichord continuo in Corelli's Op. 5 sonatas', pp. 665–79.

9   Terence Best, 'Handel's chamber music: sources, chronology and authenticity',
    EM 13 (1985), pp. 484–5.

10 Georg Muffat, *Auserlesene Instrumentalmusik* (Passau, 1701), preface.

11 Quantz, *Versuch*, trans., p. 214.

12 Judith Milhous and Curtis Price, 'Harpsichords in the London theatres,
    1696–1715', *EM* 18 (1990), pp. 38–46 and Mark W. Stahura, 'Handel and the
    orchestra' in Donald Burrows, ed., *The Cambridge companion to Handel*
    (Cambridge, 1997), pp. 238–48.

13 Stahura, 'Handel and the orchestra', pp. 246–7.

14 Ibid., esp. p. 247 and Donald Burrows, 'Handel's oratorio performances' in *The
    Cambridge companion to Handel*, pp. 262–81.

15 The case is argued at length in Dreyfus, *Bach's continuo group*.

16 Two harpsichord parts survive for each of Cantatas 195 and 201.

17 Neal Zaslaw, *Mozart's symphonies: context, performance practice, reception*
    (Oxford, 1989), p. 195.

18 See James Webster, 'On the absence of keyboard continuo in Haydn's sym-
    phonies', *EM* 18 (1990), pp. 599–608, which incorporates findings from L. F.
    Ferguson, '"Col basso" and "Generalbass" in Mozart's keyboard concertos: nota-
    tion, performance, theory and practice' (Ph.D. diss., Princeton University, 1983).

19 Webster, 'On the absence of keyboard continuo in Haydn's symphonies', pp.
    599–608.

20 Richard Maunder, *Keyboard instruments in eighteenth-century Vienna* (Oxford,
    1998), p. 117.

21 H.C. Robbins Landon, *Haydn in England 1791–1795* (London, 1976), pp. 43ff.

22 See, for example, Heinrich Christoph Koch, *Musikalisches Lexicon* (2 vols.,
    Frankfurt, 1802; R/1964), s.v. 'Flügel'.

23 Ibid.

24 See Faye Ferguson, 'Mozart's keyboard concertos: tutti notations and per-
    formance models', *Mozart-Jahrbuch* (1984/5), pp. 32–9 and Tibor Szász, 'An
    authentic Parisian source for Mozart's Piano Concerto in C major, K.246: new
    ideas on the questions of continuo and cadenzas', *EKJ* 15 (1997), pp. 7–42.

25 Tibor Szász, 'Figured bass in Beethoven's "Emperor" Concerto: basso continuo

or orchestral cues?', *EKJ* 6–7 (1988–9), pp. 5–71 and 'Beethoven's *basso continuo*: notation and performance' in Robin Stowell, ed., *Performing Beethoven* (Cambridge, 1994), pp. 1–22.

26 Szász, 'Beethoven's *basso continuo*', p. 22.

27 See, for example, Williams, *Figured bass accompaniment*, vol. I, pp. 61–2.

28 Williams, *Figured bass accompaniment*, vol. I, pp. 75ff.

29 See, in particular, Borgir, *The performance of the basso continuo*, Buelow, *Thorough-bass accompaniment* and Mortensen, '"Unerringly tasteful"?'

30 Johann David Heinichen, *Der Generalbass in der Komposition* (1728), trans. in Mortensen, '"Unerringly tasteful"?', p. 679.

31 See, for example, Poulin, ed., *J. S. Bach's precepts*.

32 See especially Arnold's remarks on p. 331 of *The art of accompaniment*.

33 Ibid., p. 344.

34 Williams, *Figured bass accompaniment*, vol. I, pp. 38ff. and Buelow, *Thorough-bass accompaniment*, pp. 176ff.

35 See Buelow, *Thorough-bass accompaniment*, pp. 182ff. and Williams, *Figured bass accompaniment*, vol. I, pp. 40ff.

36 Williams, *Figured bass accompaniment*, pp. 75ff.

37 Borgir, *The performance of the basso continuo*, pp. 149ff.

38 Williams, *Figured bass accompaniment*, pp. 48ff.

39 Ibid., p. 83.

40 Arnold, *The art of accompaniment*, pp. 469ff.

41 Mortensen, '"Unerringly tasteful"?', p. 675.

42 Rogers, *Continuo realization*, Chapter 6.

43 C. P. E. Bach, *Versuch*, trans., pp. 314, 428.

44 Arnold, *The art of accompaniment*, pp. 366–7.

45 Szász, 'Beethoven's *basso continuo*', pp. 12–13.

46 C. P. E. Bach, *Versuch*, trans., p. 422.

47 Ibid., p. 421.

48 Rogers, *Continuo realization*, pp. 109–10.

49 See Dreyfus, *Bach's continuo group*, Chapter 3, especially p. 76.

50 Quantz, *Versuch*, trans., p. 292.

51 Winton Dean, 'The performance of recitative in late Baroque opera', *ML* 58 (1977), p. 398.

52 Rogers, *Continuo realization*, pp. 134–7.

Select bibliography

Pre-1900

Adam, Louis, *Méthode de Piano du Conservatoire* (Paris, 1804; R/1974)

Bach, Carl Philipp Emanuel, *Versuch über die wahre Art das Clavier zu spielen* (2 vols., Berlin, 1753, 1762; R/1957), trans. and ed. William Mitchell (New York, 1949; R/1974)

Clementi, Muzio, *Introduction to the art of playing on the pianoforte* (London, 1801; R/1974)

Couperin, François, *L'art de toucher le clavecin* (Paris, 1716; 2/1717), trans. and ed. Mevanwy Roberts (Leipzig, 1933)

Czerny, Carl, *Vollständige theoretisch-praktische Pianoforteschule, Op. 500* (3 vols., Vienna, 1838–9) and *Supplement (oder vierter Theil) zur grossen Pianoforte Schule* (Vienna, 1846–7), trans. as *Complete theoretical and practical Pianoforte School, Op. 500* (London, 1838–9) and *Supplement to Czerny's Royal Pianoforte School* (London, 1846–7). Chapters 2 and 3 reprinted as *On the proper performance of Beethoven's works for the piano*, ed. Paul Badura-Skoda (Vienna, 1970)

Fétis, François Joseph, and Ignaz Moscheles, *Méthode des Méthodes de Piano* (Paris, 1840; R/1973)

Gasparini, Francesco, *L'armonico pratico al cimbalo* (Venice, 1708), trans. F. Stillings, (New Haven, Conn., 1963)

Hummel, Johann Nepomuk, *Ausführliche, theoretisch-practische Anweisung zum Pianoforte-Spiele* (Vienna, 1828), trans. as *A complete theoretical and practical course of instructions on the art of playing the pianoforte* (London, 1828)

Kalkbrenner, Friedrich Wilhelm Michael, *Méthode pour apprendre le pianoforte* (Paris, 1830), trans. (London, 1862)

Mace, Thomas, *Music's monument* (London, 1676; R/1958)

Marpurg, Friedrich Wilhelm, *Die Kunst das Klavier zu spielen* (Berlin, 1750, 4/1762; R(1762 edn)/1969)

Marpurg, *Anleitung zum Clavierspielen* (Berlin, 1755, 2/1765; R(1765 edn)/1969)

Milchmeyer, Johann Peter, *Die wahre Art das Pianoforte zu spielen* (Dresden, 1797)

Mozart, Leopold, *Gründliche Violinschule* (Augsburg, 1756; R(1787 edn)/1956), trans. Edith Knocker (Oxford, 2/1985)

143

Pasquali, Niccolò, *Thorough-bass made easy* (London, 1757; R/1974)

Quantz, Johann Joachim, *Versuch einer Anweisung, die Flöte traversiere zu spielen* (Berlin, 1752, 3/1789; R(1789 edn)/1952), trans. Edward R. Reilly (London, 2/1985)

Rameau, Jean-Philippe, preface to *Pièces de clavecin* (Paris, 1724), trans. and ed. Erwin R. Jacobi (Kassel, 1972)

Saint-Lambert, M. de, *Les Principes du Clavecin* (Paris, 1702; R/1974), trans. and ed. Rebecca Harris-Warrick (Cambridge, 1984)

Starke, Friedrich, *Wiener Pianoforteschule* (3 vols., Vienna, 1819–21)

Türk, Daniel Gottlob, *Klavierschule* (Leipzig and Halle, 1789, 2/1802; R(1802 edn)/1962), trans. Raymond H. Haggh (Lincoln, Nebr., 1982)

Wieck, Friedrich, *Clavier und Gesang* (Leipzig, 1853), trans. and ed. Henry Pleasants as *Piano and song* (New York, 1988)

Post-1900

Abraham, Gerald, ed., *The New Oxford history of music*, esp. vols VI–IX (London, 1973–90)

Apel, Willi, *The history of keyboard music to 1700* (Bloomington, 1972)

Apel, Willi, and John Caldwell, eds., *Corpus of early keyboard music* (American Institute of Musicology, 1963–)

Arnold, Frank T., *The art of accompaniment from a thorough-bass* (London, 1931; R/1961)

Badura-Skoda, Eva and Paul, *Mozart-Interpretation* (Vienna, 1957), trans. Leo Black as *Interpreting Mozart on the keyboard* (London, 1962; R/1986)

Bevan, Clifford, *Musical instrument collections in the British Isles* (Winchester, 1990)

Bie, Oscar, *A history of the pianoforte and pianoforte players* (London, 1899 (original German edn of 1898); R/1966)

Boalch, Donald, *Makers of the harpsichord and clavichord*, 3rd edn by Charles Mould, (Oxford, 1995)

Borgir, Tharald, *The performance of the basso continuo in Italian Baroque music* (Ann Arbor, 1987)

Brauchli, Bernard, *The clavichord* (Cambridge, 1998)

Brown, Howard Mayer, and Stanley Sadie, eds., *Performance practice: music after 1600* (London, 1989)

Buelow, George J., *Thorough-bass accompaniment according to Johann David Heinichen* (Ann Arbor, 1986)

Burrows, Donald, ed., *The Cambridge companion to Handel* (Cambridge, 1997)

Butt, John, *Bach interpretation: articulation marks in primary sources of J. S. Bach* (Cambridge, 1990)

Caldwell, John, *Editing early music* (Oxford, 1985, 2/1995)

   English keyboard music before the nineteenth century (Oxford, 1973; R/1985)

Cole, Michael, *The pianoforte in the Classical era* (Oxford, 1997)

Dale, William, *Tschudi the harpsichord maker* (London, 1913)

David, Hans T. and Arthur Mendel, *The Bach reader* (New York and London, 2/1972)

Dirksen, Peter, ed., *The harpsichord and its repertoire* (Utrecht, 1992)

Dreyfus, Laurence, *Bach's continuo group* (Cambridge, Mass., 1987)

Ehrlich, Cyril, *The piano: a history* (Oxford, 2/1990)

Eigeldinger, Jean-Jacques, *Chopin vu par ses élèves* (Neuchâtel, 1970), trans. Naomi
   Shohet, ed. Roy Howat as *Chopin: pianist and teacher* (Cambridge, 1986)

Ferguson, Howard, *Keyboard interpretation from the 14th to the 19th century: an
   introduction* (London, 2/1987)

Forbes, Eliot, ed., *Thayer's life of Beethoven* (Princeton, 2/1990)

Georgii, Walter, ed., *Four hundred years of European keyboard music* (Cologne, 1959)

Gerig, Reginald R., *Famous pianists and their technique* (Washington and New York,
   1974)

Gill, Dominic, *The book of the piano* (Oxford, 1981)

Grier, James, *The critical editing of music* (Cambridge, 1996)

Gustafson, Bruce, *French harpsichord music of the seventeenth century: a thematic
   catalog of the sources with commentary* (3 vols., Ann Arbor, Mich., 1977–9)

Gustafson, Bruce, and David Fuller, *A catalogue of French harpsichord music
   1699–1780* (Oxford, 1990)

Harding, Rosamond, *The piano-forte: its history traced to The Great Exhibition of
   1851* (Old Woking, 2/1978)

Harley, John, *British harpsichord music* (2 vols., Aldershot, 1992, 1994)

Harrison, Bernard, *Haydn's keyboard music* (Oxford, 1997)

Haskell, Harry, *The early music revival* (London, 1988)

Hefling, Stephen, *Rhythmic alteration in seventeenth- and eighteenth-century music*
   (New York, 1993)

Hubbard, Frank, *Three centuries of harpsichord making* (Cambridge, Mass., 1965)

Hudson, Richard, *Stolen time: the history of tempo rubato* (Oxford, 1994)

Jackson, Roland, *Performance practice, Medieval to contemporary: a bibliographic
   guide* (New York, 1988)

Jorgensen, Owen, *Tuning: containing the perfection of eighteenth-century temperament, the lost art of nineteenth-century temperament, and the science of equal
   temperament* (East Lansing, Mich., 1991)

   Tuning the historical temperaments by ear (Marquette, Mich., 1977)

Klop, Gerrit, *Harpsichord tuning* (Garderen, 1974)

Komlós, Katalin, *Fortepianos and their music* (Oxford, 1995)

Lawson, Colin, and Robin Stowell, *The historical performance of music: an introduction* (Cambridge, 1999)

Ledbetter, David, *Continuo playing according to Handel* (Oxford, 1990)
  Harpsichord and lute music in 17th century France (London, 1987)

Lindley, Mark, and Maria Boxall, *Early keyboard fingerings* (London, 1992)

Marshall, Robert L., ed., *Eighteenth-century keyboard music* (New York, 1994)

Maunder, Richard, *Keyboard instruments in eighteenth-century Vienna* (Oxford, 1998)

Neumann, Frederick, *Ornamentation and improvisation in Mozart* (Princeton, 1986)
  Performance practices of the seventeenth and eighteenth centuries (New York, 1993)
  The ornamentation of Baroque and post-Baroque music (Princeton, 1983)

Newman, William, *Beethoven on Beethoven: playing his piano music his way* (New York, 1988)
  The sonata in the Baroque era (New York and London, 4/1983)
  The sonata in the Classic era (New York and London, 3/1983)
  The sonata since Beethoven (New York and London, 3/1983)

O'Brien, Grant, *Ruckers: a harpsichord and virginal building tradition* (Cambridge, 1990)

Padgham, Charles, *The well-tempered organ* (Oxford, 1986)

Panetta, Vincent J., trans. and ed., *Treatise on harpsichord tuning by Jean Denis* (Cambridge, 1987)

Pollens, Stewart, *The early pianoforte* (Cambridge, 1995)

Poulin, Pamela, ed., *J. S. Bach's precepts and principles for playing the thorough-bass or accompanying in four parts* (Oxford, 1994)

Ripin, Edwin, et al., *Early keyboard instruments* (London, 1989); part of *The New Grove* musical instrument series
  The piano (London, 1988); part of *The New Grove* musical instrument series

Ripin, Edwin, ed., *Keyboard instruments: studies in keyboard organology* (Edinburgh, 1971; New York, 1977)

Rogers, Patrick J., *Continuo realization in Handel's vocal music* (Ann Arbor, 1989)

Rosenblum, Sandra, *Performance practices in Classic piano music* (Bloomington, 1991)

Rowland, David, *A history of pianoforte pedalling* (Cambridge, 1993)

Rowland, David, ed., *The Cambridge companion to the piano* (Cambridge, 1998)

Russell, Raymond, *The harpsichord and clavichord*, 2nd edn by Howard Schott (London, 1973)

Sadie, Stanley, ed., *The New Grove dictionary of music and musicians* (London, 1980)

Silbiger, Alexander, ed., *Keyboard music before 1700* (New York, 1995)
  17th century keyboard music: sources central to the keyboard art of the Baroque (24 vols., New York, 1987–9)

Stowell, Robin, ed., *Performing Beethoven* (Cambridge, 1994)

Temperley, Nicholas, *The London pianoforte school 1766–1860* (20 vols., New York and London, 1984–7)

Tilney, Colin, *The art of the unmeasured prelude* (London, 1991)

Tittle, Martin B., *A performer's guide through historical keyboard tunings* (Ann Arbor, Mich., 1978)

Todd, R. Larry, ed., *Nineteenth-century piano music* (New York, 1990)

Vinquist, Mary, and Neal Zaslaw, *Performance practice: a bibliography* (New York, 1971)

Wainwright, David, *Broadwood by appointment* (London, 1982)

Whitmore, Philip, *Unpremeditated art: the cadenza in the classical keyboard concerto* (Oxford, 1991)

Williams, Peter, *Figured-bass accompaniment* (2 vols., Edinburgh, 1970)

Williams, Peter, ed., *Bach, Handel, Scarlatti: tercentenary essays* (Cambridge, 1985)

Zaslaw, Neal, *Mozart's symphonies: context, performance practice, reception* (Oxford, 1989)

Index